EASY SOUPS FROM SCRATCH WITH QUICK BREADS TO MATCH

EASY SOUPS
FROM SCRATCH
WITH
QUICK BREADS
TO MATCH

70 recipes
to pair and share

IVY MANNING

Photographs by Dina Avila

CHRONICLE BOOKS
SAN FRANCISCO

Library of Congress Cataloging-in-
Publication Data available.

ISBN 978-1-4521-5502-9

Manufactured in China

Designed by Alice Chau
Photographs by Dina Avila
Food styling by Ashley Marti & Ivy Manning
Prop styling by Ashley Marti

10 9 8 7 6 5 4 3 2 1

Chronicle books and gifts are available
at special quantity discounts to corpora-
tions, professional associations, literacy
programs, and other organizations. For
details and discount information, please
contact our premiums department at
corporatesales@chroniclebooks.com or at
1-800-759-0190.

Chronicle Books LLC
680 Second Street
San Francisco, California 94107
www.chroniclebooks.com

*"It is impossible to think of any good meal,
no matter how plain or elegant,
without soup or bread in it."*

—M.F.K. Fisher

Introduction

CHAPTER 3:

Breads to Match 129

Introduction

I've been teaching cooking classes for over fifteen years, and some of my most popular classes focus on soups. Students tell me repeatedly that they are in need of great soup recipes—the faster the better. So over the years, I have developed scores of soup recipes that taste like they've been bubbling away for hours, but take under an hour to make. They have always been a big hit.

People loved these classes, but something always felt a bit lacking to me. My mind would wander off from the soup pot to what I'd like to crumble over the top of the soup, or dip into the bowl, or use as a sponge to sop up the last delicious bites at the bottom of the bowl. Yup, I was thinking about how homemade bread would really complete the soups and truly make them a meal.

I'm not alone in my view. Nearly every culture in the world appreciates the joy of the soup-plus-bread equation. In Ireland, you'll find that their famous lamb stew is always served with a hunk of dark Irish soda bread to sop up the last bites. Fly southeast to the eastern coast of Africa, and families are tucking into spicy red lentil stew with springy teff *injera* to scoop it up. Cross the Atlantic, and you'll see the citizens of Mexico City slurping up chile-flecked pork *posole*, a spoon in one hand and a warm, soft corn tortilla in the other.

Bread makes soup better, no matter where you live. But when I thought about including breads in my soup-making classes, I knew that my time-crunched students wouldn't use recipes that require lots of kneading, lengthy rising, and time-consuming baking. So I became expert in quick-cooking flatbreads, savory scones and muffins, and other delicious home-made breads that could be whipped up in the time it took to simmer a pot of soup, and I added them to every soup class.

My classes and the enthusiastic feedback from my pupils became the inspiration for this book. In it, you'll find forty-five recipes for easy, delicious soups and twenty-five quick bread recipes that partner perfectly with the soups to make a delicious meal. Whether you're craving a roll-up-your-sleeves supper of spicy chili with a wedge of rustic skillet corn bread, or you'd rather dip your spoon into sophisticated lobster bisque with a side of airy Gruyère cheese puffs, this book has you covered. I hope the recipes will inspire you to get your own soup and bread mojo going and make the most comforting meal of all—the one that is made with your own hands. Let's get slurping and dipping, shall we?

CHAPTER 1

Getting Started

Flavor Toolbox

Good food begins with good ingredients, and never is this more important than when making soup and bread. Over the decades, I've turned to the following ingredients to turn my soup and bread flavors up to eleven. These ingredients build flavor, balance tastes, and make the process of getting dinner on the table quicker and easier.

Anchovies (1)

If you add anchovies to aromatic vegetables when you begin cooking a soup, you will get a subtle salty-meaty base note, which will not taste fishy at all. If you include them in herb butter to brush on flatbread, they will transform it into an umami masterpiece. You'll find anchovies in recipes like the Creamy Cannellini Bean Soup with Gremolata (page 56) and Quick Flatbread made with Anchovy–Garlic Butter (page 135). The best anchovies come packed in olive oil in small glass jars. Anchovies in oil keep in the refrigerator for up to 3 months.

Demiglace Concentrate (2)

This little kitchen cheat gives quick-cooked beef and lamb soups and stews a long-simmered, beefy flavor and lip-smacking mouthfeel. Look for this very thick (gummy, even) concentrate where bouillon cubes are sold in upscale grocery stores, gourmet stores, and online. My favorite brand is More Than Gourmet Demi-Glace Gold.

Dried Mushrooms (3)

Dried mushrooms contain a high concentration of glutamic acid—nature's version of MSG—so adding them to soups is a no-brainer. I love dried porcini mushrooms for the sweet, earthy flavor they add to soup. Dried shiitake mushrooms are great for soup as well; I find that the ones available at Asian markets tend to be of better quality than the tiny bags found in grocery stores, and they are loads cheaper. Either soaked and chopped, or just thrown whole into the soup pot to enhance the broth, dried mushrooms are powerhouses of umami flavor.

Dry Sherry (4)

Spanish dry sherry is wine that is aged in partially filled casks to oxidize and intensify its flavor, and finished with a swish of brandy for extra oomph. Sherries range from flinty to nutty to sweet. Sweet cream

sherries are for old ladies to sip; for cooking, stick with dry sherry. I always have a bottle of dry oloroso sherry in the refrigerator. The complex, nutty taste adds depth to soups with earthy flavor profiles like Many Mushroom and Quinoa Soup (page 65), and it enhances creamy soups like Creamy Wild Rice and Turkey Soup (page 106). Look for sherry in the wine department of grocery stores. Sherry keeps in the refrigerator for up to 3 months.

Extra-Virgin Olive Oil (5)

I confess I've got an olive oil addiction. I've got at least five bottles going at all times. I have one big bottle of everyday extra-virgin oil for sautéing, a few herb- and citrus-infused oils, and a slew of finer oils— peppery Tuscan oil for drizzling on soups and bread, mild and buttery California oil for baking muffins, and sunny Spanish oil for salads. I prefer extra-virgin olive oil to regular olive oil, which tends to be of poor quality with off flavors. Extra-virgin olive oil is light and heat sensitive; keep it in a cool, dark place away from the stove.

Flour

Believe it or not, something as basic as which all-purpose flour you use really affects your baking results. I use unbleached all-purpose flour and favor locally milled brands over big name brands. When I want the flavor and extra fiber of whole-wheat flour, I include white whole-wheat flour in recipes. White whole-wheat flour, available in the baking aisle of most grocery stores, is made from whole kernels of hard white spring whole wheat, which makes more subtly flavored whole-wheat flour than traditional red wheat.

Fried Shallots (6)

Shelf-stable fried shallots are available in plastic containers at Asian markets. They add crunch and an oniony punch to muffins and flatbreads and are a great garnish for soups like Spicy Sweet Chicken Curry Soup (page 102). I also use them in Berbere Spice Blend (see page 51). Packaged fried shallots last indefinitely in a cool, dark pantry. You can make your own by tossing thinly sliced shallots with cornstarch and deep-frying them until golden brown; they won't last as long as the packaged variety, but they are delicious. Alternatively, substitute packaged fried onions (the type used to top old-school green bean casseroles).

Lemon Juice (7)

One of the most important tools for soup makers, lemon juice lends brightness and acidity to soup like no other ingredient. Packaged juices contain additives to extend their shelf life; perhaps that's why they taste like floor cleaner. I use freshly squeezed juice only. Since I often use the zest of the lemon and conventional lemon peels can be covered in pesticides, I buy organic lemons. (The same goes for limes.)

Miso (8)

Miso is a fermented bean-and-grain paste that is used in Japanese and Korean soups, marinades, and dressings. It comes in a variety of flavors and colors, depending on the types of beans and grains used. The most common are white (*shiro*) miso, which is slightly sweet and subtle, and the more pungent red (*aka*) miso. I use miso to boost the umami flavor of a number of soups in this book. It lasts indefinitely in the refrigerator. Miso's popularity is on the rise, so you're likely to find it at most grocery stores in the refrigerated section of the produce department.

Nutritional Yeast (9)

Also called "brewer's yeast," these bright yellow dried flakes are made from deactivated yeast, and are rich in B complex vitamins. Most folks know nutritional yeast as a salt-free sprinkle for popcorn. The buttery, cheesy flavor also enhances soups made with chicken broth and breads that can use extra richness, such as the Pilot Biscuits (page 143). You'll find nutritional yeast in bulk in health food stores, grocery stores, and online.

Packaged Broths

When it comes to making soups, the broth is the most important ingredient. Bad or weak broth can make an entire pot of soup fail. I have nothing against packaged broths, but they are not all equal, and even within a brand, the quality may vary wildly from the chicken to the beef broth. Also, note that the words *broth* and *stock* are generally used interchangeably by producers; either will work in the recipes in this book. The best tack is to try all of those available in your area until you find the ones you like. In case you want a place to start, here are my go-to packaged broths.

VEGETABLE: Imagine brand vegetarian No-Chicken broth has a light, clean flavor for lighter soups, and Pacific mushroom broth lends an earthy, rich flavor to darker vegetarian soups

SEAFOOD OR CLAM: Bar Harbor seafood stock and clam stock have loads of seafood flavor without tons of salt.

CHICKEN: Pacific organic chicken broth has a light, fairly neutral flavor, so your soup ingredients will be the main focus, not the broth.

BEEF: Rachael Ray brand beef stock delivers rich, beefy flavor without the metallic tang of rival brands.

Parmigiano-Reggiano (10)

When I call for Parmesan cheese, I mean imported Parmigiano-Reggiano cheese. Full of natural umami-giving glutamates and rich, sweet, nutty flavor, it's my favorite tool of all. Once I've grated it down to the hard rind of the cheese, I use the rind just as I would a bay leaf, to infuse soups with flavor. Parmigiano-Reggiano cheese and its rind will keep in the refrigerator for up to 4 months, though they are best used within 2 months.

Salt (11)

I use fine sea salt for seasoning and baking. Generally, I season soup with salt only after the soup is done. That's because as it simmers, steam escapes and the soup reduces, becoming saltier and more concentrated. I also use fine sea salt for baking breads and muffins, but to finish breads, I use coarse sea salt, such as Maldon, because the flaky texture adds crunch.

Soy Sauce (12)

I use naturally fermented and aged soy sauce (*shoyu*) to give soups a full, rounded saltiness, plus umami. My favorite brand is Ohsawa, which you can find at Asian markets and natural food stores. Ohsawa also makes gluten-free tamari, a perfect substitute if you're sensitive or allergic to wheat gluten.

Truffle Oil

Truffle oil is a divisive issue among chefs and foodies because most brands rely on synthetic compounds to mimic the buttery, funky flavor of the pricey fungus. Personally, I find the flavor of good-quality truffle oil to be a most welcome addition to vegetable and Italian-style bean soups like Broken Pasta and Bean Soup (page 71). Just a drizzle at the end of cooking can add loads of flavor. Besides, I can rarely afford real truffles. Look for truffle oil made with extra-virgin olive oil; a small bottle will last for 3 months when stored in a cool, dry place.

Water

If your tap water isn't clean and clear tasting enough to drink, then it's not good enough for your soup, either. If you buy bottled water or filter your tap water for drinking, use the same water in your soup. If you are lucky enough to live in a place where the tap water is delicious, as it is in the Pacific Northwest, where I live, then use that.

The Three B's: Broths, Beans, and One Very Versatile Bread Dough

There are three "b's" that form the backbone of many of the soup-and-bread meals in this book. Broth—vegetable, chicken, or beef—is the liquid of choice in most of my soup recipes; beans add protein and flavor; and my versatile olive oil bread dough is utilized in several bread recipes within these pages. In this section, I'll show you how to take the reins and make these essentials from scratch.

Broth

The old adage "the better the broth, the better the soup" is true. Sure, you can use canned broth or stock. But if you've got a slow cooker or a soup pot, making home-made broth is as easy as boiling water, and the payback for letting a pot of homemade broth bubble away for a few hours is great: Your home will smell absolutely wonderful and your soups will have a deep, rich homemade flavor. You'll also be consuming a healthier food—homemade broths have a fraction of the sodium of packaged broths.

I've found that simmering ingredients over low heat for a long time produces the most flavorful broths, so I use my slow cooker, which requires minimal work. If you don't have one, see the stove-top variation at the end of each broth recipe.

Vegetable Broth

If you don't mind a dark broth, add 8 oz [230 g] of cremini mushrooms to this mixture of vegetables for added depth.

MAKES 12 CUPS [2.8 L]
ACTIVE TIME 10 MINUTES
TOTAL TIME 8 TO 9 HOURS

2 medium yellow onions, coarsely chopped, with skins
2 large leeks, white and green parts, halved lengthwise, rinsed, and coarsely chopped
3 large carrots, coarsely chopped
3 large celery stalks, coarsely chopped
1 small fennel bulb, chopped
4 large garlic cloves, coarsely chopped
1 Tbsp tomato paste
8 black peppercorns
6 fresh thyme sprigs
2 bay leaves
1 Tbsp soy sauce

1. In a 7-qt/6.5-L slow cooker, combine the onions, leeks, carrots, celery, fennel, garlic, tomato paste, peppercorns, thyme, and bay leaves. Cover with 12 cups [2.8 L] of cold water. Cover the cooker and cook on low heat for 8 to 9 hours.

2. Strain the broth through a fine-mesh sieve into a large bowl. Add the soy sauce. Refrigerate, uncovered, until the broth has cooled completely. Store in airtight containers in the refrigerator for up to 4 days, or in the freezer for up to 3 months.

STOVE-TOP VARIATION: Combine the onions, leeks, carrots, celery, fennel, garlic, tomato paste, peppercorns, thyme, and bay leaves in a large soup pot. Add 12 cups [2.8 L] of cold water and bring to a boil over high heat. Reduce the heat to low, cover, and simmer gently for 1½ hours. Strain and add the soy sauce. Refrigerate and store as directed above.

Chicken Broth

The chicken meat can be picked off the bones and reserved for another use once the broth is done cooking.

MAKES 12 CUPS [2.8 L]
ACTIVE TIME 10 MINUTES
TOTAL TIME 8 TO 9 HOURS

One 5- to 6-lb [2.3- to 2.7-kg] chicken, cut into eighths
2 large carrots, coarsely chopped
2 large celery stalks, coarsely chopped
1 large yellow onion, coarsely chopped, with skins
8 black peppercorns
2 bay leaves
2 sprigs fresh thyme

1. In a 7-qt/6.5-L slow cooker, combine all the ingredients. Cover with 12 cups [2.8 L] of cold water. Cover the cooker and cook on low heat for 8 to 9 hours.

2. Strain the broth through a fine-mesh sieve into a large bowl. Refrigerate the broth, uncovered, until cool. Spoon off and discard the hard fat that has settled on the top of the broth. Store in airtight containers in the refrigerator for up to 4 days, or in the freezer for up to 3 months.

STOVE-TOP VARIATION: Combine the ingredients in a large soup pot. Add 12 cups [2.8 L] of cold water and bring to a boil over high heat. Reduce the heat to low, cover, and simmer gently for 1½ hours. Strain the broth, refrigerate, skim, and store as directed above.

Beef Broth

Ever the frugal cook, I pull the meat from the long-stewed bones in this recipe and add it to marinara to make a Sicilian-style ragu.

MAKES 10 CUPS [2.4 L]
ACTIVE TIME 15 MINUTES
TOTAL TIME 8 TO 9 HOURS

5 lb [2.3 kg] meaty beef bones
    (a mix of oxtails, knuckle bones,
    and shank bones)
2 large carrots, coarsely chopped
2 large celery stalks, coarsely
    chopped
1 large yellow onion, coarsely
    chopped, with skins
2 Tbsp tomato paste
10 black peppercorns
2 bay leaves
6 sprigs fresh thyme

1. Adjust an oven rack so that it is 6 in [15 cm] below the heating element, and preheat the broiler on high. Line a rimmed baking sheet with aluminum foil.

2. Arrange the beef bones in an even layer on the prepared baking sheet. Broil until the tops are browned, 6 to 8 minutes. Flip the bones with tongs and broil on the second side until well browned, 5 minutes more.

3. In a 7-qt/6.5-L slow cooker, combine the bones with the carrots, celery, onion, tomato paste, peppercorns, bay leaves, and thyme. Cover with 8 cups [2 L] of cold water. Cover the cooker and cook on low heat for 8 to 9 hours.

4. Strain the broth through a fine-mesh sieve into a large bowl. Refrigerate the broth, uncovered, until cool. Spoon off and discard the hard fat that has settled on top of the broth. Store in airtight containers in the refrigerator for up to 4 days, or in the freezer for up to 3 months.

STOVE-TOP VARIATION: Broil the bones as instructed above. Combine the broiled bones, carrots, celery, onion, tomato paste, peppercorns, bay leaves, and thyme in a large soup pot. Add 8 cups [2 L] of cold water and bring to a boil over high heat. Reduce heat to low, cover, and simmer gently for 3 hours. Strain the broth, refrigerate, skim, and store as directed above.

Cooking Beans from Scratch

Bean	Quantity Dried	Slow-Cooker Cooking Time	Yield
Black	3 cups [550 g]	8 to 9 hours	8 cups [1.4 kg]
Black-Eyed Peas	3 cups [530 g]	5 to 6 hours	8 cups [1.3 kg]
Cannellini	3 cups [565 g]	7 to 8 hours	8½ cups [1.3 kg]
Cranberry/Borlotti	3 cups [570 g]	8 to 9 hours	8 cups [1.4 kg]
Kidney (see Note)	3 cups [490 g]	6 to 7 hours	7 cups [1.2 kg]
Small Red	3 cups [515 g]	7 to 8 hours	7 cups [1.2 kg]

Note: Slow-cooking dried beans works well for all beans except kidney beans. Kidney beans contain a high concentration of phytohaemagglutinin (also called "kidney bean lectin"). This chemical is toxic to our tummies and will cause food poisoning–like symptoms if not boiled briskly. If you are going to cook dried or even soaked-overnight kidney beans in a slow cooker, you absolutely must boil them for 15 minutes and drain them before they go in the machine.

How to Make the Best Homemade Beans

The best-tasting beans are homemade. Generally, I use homemade beans in my soups because it's as easy as turning on a slow cooker. Plus, beans freeze really well, so it's easy to make a big batch and bank some for later. (Don't worry if you don't have home-cooked beans around; I include instructions in recipes for using canned beans as well.)

Personally, I think the best-tasting home-made beans are made from dried beans that have not been soaked overnight. Conventional wisdom used to dictate that soaking dried beans before cooking them makes them easier to digest and quicker to cook, but recent studies have confirmed that there is no science to back this up. Hurrah, one less step!

I've cooked thousands of batches of beans, and I've found that the easiest and tastiest way to prepare dried beans is to chuck them in a slow cooker, add water and a few aromatics, and let them cook slowly on low heat for several hours. The finished beans have a plump, but not mushy, texture and tons of bean-y flavor. Every few weeks, I make a batch of beans and freeze them to use later in soups. In case you don't have a slow cooker, I've included a quick stove-top recipe, too.

Dried beans vary greatly in cooking time, depending on what type of beans you are using, how old the beans are, and how hard or soft your water is. I supply a range of cooking times (see the chart on page 18); start checking your beans at the low end of the suggested cooking time, and go from there. Also, keep in mind that not all slow cookers are created equal. Your mom's harvest-orange slow cooker from the '70s cooks at a significantly cooler temperature [about 25°F or -4°C] than newer units.

No-Soak Slow-Cooker Beans

MAKES 7 TO 10 CUPS [1.2 TO 1.7 KG]
ACTIVE TIME 10 MINUTES
TOTAL TIME 5 TO 9 HOURS

3 cups [515 to 570 g] dried beans
   (see chart on page 18)
½ medium yellow onion, chopped
   (optional)
1 medium garlic clove, peeled
   (optional)
2 tsp sea salt
1 bay leaf

1. Rinse the beans and pick out any stones or shriveled beans. Drain the beans and add to a 3- to 7-qt/3.5- to 6.5-L slow cooker. Add the onion and garlic (if using), the salt, the bay leaf, and enough cold water to cover the beans by 2 in [5 cm], or about 8 cups [2 L]). Cover the cooker and cook on low heat until the beans are tender, 5 to 9 hours, depending on the age of the beans and your slow cooker.

2. Drain any remaining liquid from the beans, transfer to a large bowl, and cool completely in the refrigerator. Store in an airtight container in the refrigerator for up to 3 days. Or divide into 1½-cup [255-g] portions and store in zip-top plastic freezer bags in the freezer for up to 3 months. (Lay the bags flat for efficient storage.)

STOVE-TOP VARIATION: Prepare the beans for cooking as directed above, and combine the ingredients in a large soup pot. Add enough cold water to cover by 4 in [10 cm], or about 8 cups [2 L]). Bring to a boil over high heat, cover, and reduce the heat to maintain a gentle simmer. Cook until the beans are tender, 45 minutes to 1½ hours. Drain, cool, and store as directed above.

Fast, Adaptable Yeast-Risen Dough

I love to bake fresh bread, but bread dough made with yeast requires lots of time to rise, time I don't always have to spare. So I've developed a recipe for fast-rising dough that I use for a number of different applications in this book—Olive and Prosciutto Rolls (page 163), Roasted Garlic Focaccia (page 142), and Thin and Crispy Breadsticks (page 144). Just mix, form into the desired shape, and let it rise for 30 minutes. Then it's ready for the oven!

Not only is this dough versatile and fast, but it also doubles well so you can freeze half for another baking project later.

Fresh-and-Fast Olive Oil Bread Dough

MAKES ABOUT 1 LB [455 G], ENOUGH FOR 12 ROLLS, 1 FOCACCIA BREAD, OR ABOUT 72 BREADSTICKS
ACTIVE TIME 10 MINUTES
TOTAL TIME 15 MINUTES

¾ cup [180 ml] warm water (105°F [40°C])
1½ tsp honey
2¼ tsp active dry yeast
1½ Tbsp extra-virgin olive oil
1½ cups [210 g] all-purpose flour
½ cup [70 g] white whole-wheat flour
¾ tsp sea salt

1. In a large bowl, combine the water and the honey and stir to dissolve. Sprinkle the yeast over the water and let it sit for 5 minutes. Add the olive oil and whisk to combine. Add both flours and the salt and stir with a wooden spoon until the mixture becomes a sticky mass, about 1 minute. Transfer the dough to a stand mixer fitted with a dough hook and knead on medium speed until smooth and elastic, about 4 minutes. (Alternatively, knead by hand on a lightly floured surface until smooth and elastic, 8 minutes.)

2. Use immediately in a recipe, or flatten into a 6-in [15-cm] disk and freeze in a zip-top plastic freezer bag for up to 3 months. Defrost overnight in the refrigerator before using.

Safety: A Note on Safely Storing and Reheating Soups

Most of the soups in this book can be made in advance and frozen. Before you transfer the soup to storage containers, though, it's important to cool it down quickly to get it out of the "danger zone," between 40° and 140°F [4° and 60°C], where bacteria multiply rapidly.

To cool soup down swiftly, transfer it from the pot to a large bowl. From this point, you have two choices: either set the bowl of hot soup in a larger bowl full of ice water, or plunge an ice paddle into the center of the soup. Refrigerate either setup until the soup is cold to the touch. Heavy plastic ice paddles can be purchased at kitchen stores, or you can make your own by filling a sturdy plastic bottle three-fourths full with water, capping it, and freezing it until solid. Wash and refreeze the paddle between uses.

Once the soup is 39°F [3.9°C] or colder, store it in 1-qt [960-ml] zip-top freezer bags (they're great space savers because they lie flat in the freezer) or in 1-qt [960-ml] plastic or glass containers. Even the toughest plastic containers break down with time, and extreme temperatures and can lead to chemicals leaching into your food. I use glass containers to store soup instead. When filling containers with cooled soup, leave at least ½ in [12 mm] of space at the top, so there is room for the soup to expand as it freezes.

The next step is to label and date the containers. I know what you're thinking: it's obvious what's in there. You'll remember. I speak from experience here; it won't be obvious what soup is in which container in a few months, and I promise you, you'll forget. For the sake of your safety and your sanity, invest in a Sharpie marker and a roll of easy-to-remove blue painter's masking tape and write down the contents of each container and when you froze it.

The best way to defrost frozen soup is to place it in the refrigerator and let it come back to life overnight. This way, vegetables will retain more of their texture, beans won't get mushy, and meat and seafood won't break down as much. Never defrost soup at room temperature (remember the danger zone?). To defrost soup more quickly, heat soup on the low setting in the microwave in 2- to 3-minute bursts until it is slushy. Then reheat it on high heat. If you must reheat frozen soup on the stove top, add a bit of broth or water to the bottom of the pan, cover, and warm the soup over low heat, stirring frequently to reduce the chances of scorching.

Once the soup is hot, taste it. The flavors of soup fade with time in the freezer; so you may need to add salt, freshly ground pepper, fresh herbs, or a squeeze of lemon juice to rejuvenate the soup before putting it on the table.

CHAPTER 2

Soups
from
Scratch

Soups

In this chapter, we will dive into the steamy, slurpy, satisfying world of soups. There is a perception that soups are difficult to master; perhaps that is because soups tend to have a longer list of ingredients than other recipes. In reality, cooking a pot of soup from scratch is just a matter of a shopping well and following a few simple techniques like sautéing, browning, and simmering. In the following sections, I'll show you how to make amazing soups that taste deceptively complex but take less than an hour from start to finish.

As half of a mixed-diet family and someone who followed a gluten-free diet for a time because of health concerns, I'm acutely aware of the need for adaptable, flexible recipes. Throughout this book, I note substitutions wherever possible to make the recipes gluten-free, vegetarian, or vegan. Often, it's a matter of one quick substitution to make a dish acceptable for everyone at the table, and that's certainly worth doing in the interest of dinner table harmony.

To start off this chapter, I offer up ten time-saving tips that will change how you approach soup (and possibly cooking in general) forever. And since we all hit a road bump in the kitchen now and then, I've also included a little troubleshooting section to help you fix any problems you might encounter on your journey to a great bowl of soup.

Armed with this knowledge, we'll dive into the recipes. I start with vegetable-centric soups because much of my cooking begins with seasonal vegetables. Sprinkled throughout this group of recipes, you'll find tricks and tips for buying and preparing vegetables efficiently so you won't spend hours at the cutting board. From a creamy Roasted Asparagus Soup with Cashew Cream (page 30), which happens to be vegan, to a zesty Korean Kimchi and Tofu Soup (page 37), getting your daily recommended servings of veggies will be a breeze.

Next you'll find a fine mix of soups that feature beans and grains. By using quick-cooking grains like quinoa and pearled barley and homemade (or canned) beans, the healthful soups in this section are perfect for busy weeknights. You'll find perfected classics like Farro Minestrone (page 66) plus some exotic recipes from farther afield like Spicy Ethiopian Red Lentil Soup (page 51) and Persian Yogurt, Lentil, and Bulgur Soup drizzled with browned butter (page 62)—a soup so delicious and impressive looking, it will steal the show at your next dinner party.

Seafood is by its delicate nature a quick-cooking protein, so that's why the recipes in the next grouping come together so very fast. There's a trio of chowders, including an award-winning creamy clam chowder and a Brazilian coconut-based chowder; a couple of simple but inventive bisques; and a few little shellfish numbers, like Spicy Sicilian Clam Soup with Fregola (page 82) and Mussel Stew with Bacon, Cider, and Cream (page 89), which will keep all of you seafood lovers smiling for days.

Finally, we'll switch gears and turn to meat- and poultry-based soups and stews. From an ace recipe for a classic chicken soup—Soulful Chicken Soup (page 96), best enjoyed with light, herby dumplings—to herbal Thai Coconut Chicken Soup (page 98) and zesty Mexican Chicken Noodle Soup (page 100), this section reveals flavorful variations on the cure for the common cold. For even heartier fare, there is a tempting collection of beef-, lamb-, and pork-based soups and stews. Think intensely meaty Fast Irish Stew (page 125), inspired by the recipe served in my family's Irish pub; lightning-fast Barbecue Pork and Miso Ramen (page 118), which rivals the fare at any trendy ramen house; and a beautiful *harira*, Lamb Meatball, Garbanzo Bean, Lentil, and Tomato Soup (page 122). There's a bowl of soup for every occasion in the following pages, and plenty of recipes that I know will become firm favorites.

10 Ways to Make Soup Faster

1. THINK AHEAD. Working a bit ahead can save you headaches later. For instance, if you're going to chop some garlic for tonight's soup and you know that you'll be using more garlic later in the week, peel a whole head of garlic and throw it in a mini food processor. Keep chopped garlic in an airtight glass container in the refrigerator for up to a week. FYI: One medium garlic clove yields 1 tsp of minced garlic.

2. DO MORE THAN ONE THING AT A TIME. Think like a chef and chop the vegetables while you heat the oil in the pot. Sauté the onions while you are mincing the garlic. While the soup simmers, grate the cheese you'll use for the garnish and chop the fresh herbs. Or better yet, make a batch of bread, muffins, or rolls from chapter 3. This is how chefs get a lot done in a short amount of time.

3. LEARN HOW TO CHOP AN ONION. You'll do it over and over if you make soup frequently, so why not learn the most efficient way to chop an onion, if you haven't already? Take a knife skills class; it's the gift that keeps giving!

4. BUY PRECUT VEGETABLES. Many grocery stores sell a variety of seeded, chopped, and prepped vegetables in their produce department. These shortcuts can be great time savers. (The only exception is prechopped onions, which become acrid and watery.) And hit the salad bar; you will often find chopped vegetables and precooked grains and beans, too. Double time-saving bonus!

5. PRECOOK BEANS AND FREEZE THEM. Store drained precooked beans flat in zip-top plastic bags in 1½-cup [500- to 570-g] portions (the amount in an average can of beans). Add them directly to soup.

6. USE FRESH HERBS. When you're working fast, you don't have time to simmer the flavor out of dried herbs, so opt for fresh. For the quickest plucking of woody herbs, hold the tougher end of the herb sprig with the fingertips of one hand and with the other, gently pinch the stem while pulling downward toward the tip to "unzip" the leaves from the stem. If you bought a big bunch at the farmers' market and have leftover herbs, set the stems in a small glass of water, cover loosely with a plastic bag, and refrigerate.

7. LINE IT UP. Riffling around in the produce drawer, searching for the can opener, or washing the cutting board in the middle of the cooking process slows you down. Put all the ingredients and equipment out on the counter before you start.

8. BROWN MEAT UNDER A BROILER. Broiling, instead of browning meat on the stove top, will save you a lot of time. While the meat for your soup is broiling, you can be sautéing vegetables to get the rest of the soup started.

9. USE HOT BROTH OR WATER. Hit the ground running by adding hot broth or water to the soup pot instead of cold liquid. It can speed up the cooking time by about 10 minutes. The only exceptions for this would be soups that include very firm vegetables, such as potatoes, that are not sautéed first. These veggies will cook evenly only when started in cold or room-temperature liquid.

10. USE QUICK-COOKING GRAINS. I love whole grains, but they take a long time to cook. The recipes in this book call for quick-cooking grains like quinoa, pearled barley, bulgur, and rice, all of which cook in 45 minutes or less.

Troubleshooting Soups

All of the recipes in this book will give you tasty results, but ingredients differ, stoves differ, and every cook has a bad day now and then. It helps to know how to fix a problem, should you ever run into one. Here are some of the frequent slings and arrows of soup making and how to fix them.

PROBLEM: "My soup tastes flat."

SOLUTION: Add an acidic ingredient. Chefs know that a squeeze of lemon juice, a hit of good-quality sherry vinegar or white wine vinegar, or a glug of brandy can brighten the flavor of any dish, especially soup. Add a small amount, 1 tsp or so, to start. Taste the soup, and then add more if needed.

PROBLEM: "My soup needs salt."

SOLUTION: The obvious answer is to add salt, but there are plenty of other ingredients that can add saltiness and an interesting flavor at the same time. Specialty salts add the sodium you're looking for with other interesting notes—try smoked salt, truffle salt, or lemon salt. Fish sauce and soy sauce will also add umami, the fifth taste (in addition to sweet, sour, bitter, and salty), which lends a savory flavor and saltiness. Or whisk a little miso with a ladleful of the soup, and add the mixture to the pot for saltiness, umami, and body. Dry cheeses like Parmigiano-Reggiano, Pecorino Romano, Manchego, and dry (aged) Jack cheese will also provide saltiness, but are best added right before serving.

Sometimes, salt isn't the problem; it's actually flavor you're missing. Try adding 2 to 3 tsp of nutritional yeast (see Flavor Toolbox, page 12) or fresh herbs to heighten the flavor of a soup that lacks interest.

PROBLEM: "My soup is too salty."

SOLUTION: The best remedy is prevention. When finishing soup, taste three spoonfuls before adding any seasoning. I ladle out that much into a small ramekin, let it cool for a few seconds, and then taste it. This bigger trial size will give you a better picture of what it will be like to eat a whole bowl of the soup, so you'll be able to gauge how much salt it really needs.

If, despite your best efforts, you're stuck with a too-salty soup, add some hot water or milk, but not broth. Broth has sodium in it and will make your soup thinner, but not necessarily less salty. Contrary to soup lore, I have never found that adding a potato to the pot does anything to fix salty soup.

PROBLEM: "I want my soup to be thicker."

SOLUTION: Try simmering the soup, uncovered, to let some steam escape, thereby reducing the liquid. Or, you can purée some of the soup in a blender and return it to the pot. This will help to thicken the soup.

Another option is to add a starch. Make a slurry by whisking equal parts of all-purpose flour and water (about 1 Tbsp of each). Add this to the soup, and simmer for at least 1 minute to cook the starchiness out. You can also make a gluten-free slurry with cornstarch or arrowroot. Steer away from arrowroot if your soup contains milk or cream, however, as it makes creamy soups slimy.

Yet another option is to add pasta or rice to the soup. A handful of rice or small pasta (such as stars or couscous) will absorb some of the excess moisture and add starch to the soup, which will thicken it.

PROBLEM: "My soup tastes burned."

SOLUTION: Creamy soups, like chowders, and thick soups, such as those based on beans or lentils, can scorch easily. Prevention is the best practice. Use a heavy-bottomed soup pot; stir frequently, especially into the bottom edges of the pan; and mind the heat. Creamy soups should never cook above a gentle simmer.

If your soup has a burned, smoky taste from scorched ingredients, I'm afraid it's time to start over or order take-out.

PROBLEM: "I defrosted frozen soup and now it looks curdled."

SOLUTION: The proteins in dairy can curdle when frozen and reheated. The soup will still be delicious, but if you're a stickler for texture, strain the broth into a blender, reserving the solids, and blend it until smooth. Gently reheat the broth with the solids over low heat.

Vegetable-Centric Soups

I'm not a big fan of cold soups, but I make an exception for this zippy Spanish number. It takes a minute to make in a blender, uses up the inevitable glut of late-summer garden veggies, and is a great start to an alfresco dinner party in the dog days of summer. Since this recipe is so simple, it's best to splurge on high-end extra-virgin olive oil, real Spanish sherry vinegar, and buttery imported Marcona almonds; you will taste the difference. Instead of plain tomato juice, I like the complexity of salty-sweet V8 vegetable juice.

SERVES

6

ACTIVE TIME

20

MINUTES

TOTAL TIME

40

MINUTES

Blender Gazpacho

PAIR WITH

Thin and Crispy Breadsticks (PAGE 144)

1 medium cucumber, halved
  and seeded
1 medium red bell pepper, seeded
1 large heirloom tomato, cored
  and cut into chunks
½ medium sweet onion, peeled
  and cut into chunks
5 cups [1.2 L] canned or bottled
  tomato juice or tomato-based
  vegetable juice
1 medium garlic clove, peeled
  and chopped (see Note)
3 Tbsp Spanish sherry vinegar
2 Tbsp extra-virgin olive oil
½ tsp smoked paprika
Sea salt
Freshly ground black pepper
½ cup [70 g] chopped
  Marcona almonds

1. Finely chop enough of the cucumber, bell pepper, tomato, and onion to make 1 cup [200 g] for the garnish and set aside in the refrigerator.

2. In a blender, combine the remaining cucumber, bell pepper, tomato, and onion with the tomato juice, garlic, vinegar, olive oil, and smoked paprika. Blend until smooth (you may need to do this in batches). Season with salt and pepper. Chill for 20 minutes to allow the flavors to meld.

3. Ladle the soup into chilled bowls and garnish with the reserved vegetables and the almonds. Serve immediately.

Note: If there is a green sprout in the center of the garlic clove, remove and discard it. Since the garlic is consumed raw, the sprout may give you heartburn.

GET AHEAD: Store the soup and vegetable garnishes separately in airtight containers in the refrigerator for up to 2 days. Whisk the soup or blend it in a blender if it has separated before serving.

SERVES

4 TO 6

ACTIVE TIME

15
MINUTES

TOTAL TIME

40
MINUTES

This is my antidote to the end of winter, when I'm longing for the budding green flavors of spring. To infuse the soup with lots of asparagus flavor, I simmer the woody stems in broth before puréeing the broth with roasted asparagus spears and sautéed aromatic vegetables. This soup is creamy, but there's no cream in it. Instead, it contains cashew cream, made with roasted cashews blended with hot water. Cashew cream has the same viscosity as cream and lends the soup a nutty richness without dairy.

Roasted Asparagus Soup with Cashew Cream

PAIR WITH

Spinach and Sun-Dried Tomato Scones (PAGE 154)
Zucchini, Feta, and Dill Muffins (PAGE 168)

½ cup [70 g] roasted, salted cashews
2 lb [910 g] asparagus spears, rinsed well
5 cups [1.2 L] vegetable or chicken broth (see page 17)
2½ Tbsp extra-virgin olive oil
2 medium leeks, white and light green parts only, rinsed well and thinly sliced
1 small yellow onion, chopped
1 medium garlic clove, minced
½ cup [120 ml] dry white wine
½ cup [15 g] lightly packed baby spinach
2 tsp freshly squeezed lime juice
¼ tsp freshly grated nutmeg
Pinch of cayenne pepper
Sea salt
Freshly ground black pepper

1. In a blender, combine the cashews and ½ cup [120 ml] hot water, and blend until smooth, scraping down the sides of the blender once. Set aside.

2. Preheat the oven to 425°F [220°C]. Line a rimmed baking sheet with parchment paper.

3. Snap off the woody part of each asparagus spear by holding the spear at each end and bending it until it snaps in two. Place the woody ends in a large soup pot or Dutch oven. Add the broth to the pot, cover, and bring to a boil over high heat. Reduce the heat to medium-low and simmer, covered, for 10 minutes to extract the flavor from the asparagus ends. Strain the broth into a large bowl and discard the woody ends. Wipe out the pot.

4. While the broth simmers, place the asparagus spears on the prepared baking sheet, toss with 1 Tbsp of the olive oil, and arrange in an even layer. Roast until the spears are lightly browned and tender, 8 to 15 minutes, depending on the thickness of the spears. With scissors, clip 2 in [5 cm] off the tips of a handful of spears and set them aside for a garnish.

5. Return the pot to medium heat and add the remaining 1½ Tbsp olive oil. Add the leeks and onion and sauté until they are tender but not browned, about 4 minutes. Add the garlic and sauté for 45 seconds. Add the wine and roasted asparagus spears, increase the heat to medium-high, and boil, stirring frequently, until the wine has evaporated, about 2 minutes. Add the strained broth, stopping before you reach any grit that may have settled in the bottom of the bowl. Bring the mixture to a gentle simmer and cook, uncovered, until the asparagus is very soft, 10 minutes. Add the spinach, stir, and cook for 1 minute.

6. Purée the soup in the pot with an immersion blender, or in batches in a blender with the lid slightly ajar to allow steam to escape. Return the soup to the pot and place over low heat. Add the cashew cream, lime juice, nutmeg, and cayenne. Season with salt and pepper.

7. Ladle the soup into bowls and garnish with the reserved asparagus tips. Serve immediately.

GET AHEAD: Store the cashew cream in an airtight container in the refrigerator for up to 5 days. Allow the cream to return to room temperature before using. The finished soup, without the asparagus garnish, can be stored in airtight containers and refrigerated for up to 4 days or frozen for up to 3 months. Defrost overnight in the refrigerator and reheat gently over low heat.

SERVES

4 TO 6

ACTIVE TIME

15
MINUTES

TOTAL TIME

45
MINUTES

This vivid bowl of beet and carrot purée with a swirl of creamy Greek yogurt on top looks like spa food, but it's actually very satisfying. To make the preparation superfast, I use prepeeled baby carrots and roasted and peeled beets (look for them in the produce section or in salad bars). I've included a quick method for cooking the beets in the microwave in case you'd like to roast the beets yourself. To make this soup vegan, substitute cashew cream (see page 30) for the yogurt.

The muffins with zucchini and feta on page 168 or the corn muffins on page 167 offer a lovely salty counterpoint to the sweet, earthy flavors in this soup.

Roasted Beet and Carrot Soup

PAIR WITH

Zucchini, Feta, and Dill Muffins (PAGE 168)
Gluten-Free Corn Muffins (PAGE 167)

2 Tbsp extra-virgin olive oil
1 medium yellow onion, chopped
12 oz [340 g] baby carrots, chopped
3 medium garlic cloves, minced
5 cups [1.2 L] vegetable or
    chicken broth (see page 17)
12 oz [340 g] roasted and peeled
    beets, chopped
2 tsp ground coriander
1 Tbsp white miso
1 Tbsp freshly squeezed lemon juice
Sea salt
Freshly ground black pepper
½ cup [120 g] plain Greek yogurt

1. Heat the oil in a large soup pot or Dutch oven over medium-high heat. Add the onion and the carrots and sauté, stirring occasionally, until the onion is translucent, about 5 minutes. Add the garlic and cook until fragrant, about 45 seconds. Add the vegetable broth, beets, and coriander. Cover and bring to a simmer. Reduce the heat to low and simmer, stirring occasionally, until the carrots and beets are very tender, 20 to 30 minutes.

2. Add the miso and lemon juice to the pot. Purée in the pot with an immersion blender or in batches in a blender, with the lid slightly ajar, until smooth. Season with salt and pepper.

3. Ladle the soup into bowls and dollop with the yogurt. Serve immediately.

GET AHEAD: If you prefer to roast and peel your own beets, wash 1 lb [455 g] of raw beets. Wrap each one individually in parchment paper and place on a microwave-safe plate. Microwave on high until a paring knife slides easily into the center of a beet, 7 to 10 minutes. Let the beets stand, still wrapped in parchment, for 10 minutes. (Alternatively, wrap the beets individually in foil and roast in a 400°F [200°C] oven until a paring knife slides easily into the center of the largest beet, about 1 hour.) When cool enough to handle, push the peels off the beets with your fingers. Store in an airtight container in the refrigerator for up to 1 week.

SERVES

4 TO 6

ACTIVE TIME

15

MINUTES

TOTAL TIME

45

MINUTES

To make the perfect tomato soup, I start with canned San Marzano tomatoes, a high-quality Italian variety that packs fresh, sweet-sharp flavor like no other canned tomato. Broiling the tomatoes intensifies their flavor and adds a savory smokiness so reminiscent of bacon that my vegetarian husband was suspicious the first time he tried this soup. It's meat-free, I swear! In fact, you could make the soup vegan by using olive oil in place of the butter and omitting the cream or replacing it with the cashew cream on page 30.

For full-on tomato soup and grilled cheese nostalgia, serve this soup with a cheesy bread or biscuit (see page 157 or 160).

Smoky San Marzano Tomato Soup

PAIR WITH

Beer and Cheddar Bread (PAGE 157)
Pimento Cheese Drop Biscuits (PAGE 160)
Spinach and Sun-Dried Tomato Scones (PAGE 154)

**Two 28-oz [794-g] cans whole
San Marzano tomatoes with juice**
Sea salt
3 Tbsp unsalted butter
3 large shallots, chopped
1 Tbsp chopped fresh thyme
1 Tbsp tomato paste
2 Tbsp all-purpose flour
**4 cups [960 ml] vegetable broth
(see page 17)**
½ cup [120 ml] heavy cream
Freshly ground black pepper

1. Adjust the oven rack so that it is 3 in [7.5 cm] below the heating element, and preheat the broiler. Line a rimmed baking sheet with aluminum foil and coat with cooking spray.

2. Tear the tomatoes in half with your fingers, letting the juices drip back into the can. Set the juices aside. Arrange the tomatoes in a single layer on the prepared baking sheet and sprinkle with ¾ tsp salt. Broil, rotating the pan once, until the tomatoes are blackened in places, about 10 minutes.

3. While the tomatoes are broiling, melt the butter in a large soup pot or Dutch oven over medium heat. Add the shallots and thyme and sauté until the shallots are translucent, about 5 minutes. Add the tomato paste and flour and cook, stirring constantly, for 1 minute.

4. Add the reserved tomato juices and the vegetable broth to the pot, increase the heat to medium-high, and bring to a simmer. Reduce the heat to low and simmer, uncovered, stirring occasionally, until the tomatoes are ready. Add them to the pot, scraping up any browned bits stuck to the foil, and simmer, uncovered, for 20 minutes more.

5. Blend the soup in the pot with an immersion blender, or in batches in a blender with the lid slightly ajar and return the soup to the pot. Add the cream, and cook over medium-low heat until bubbly, about 2 minutes. Season with salt and pepper.

6. Ladle the soup into bowls, and serve immediately.

GET AHEAD: This recipe freezes well and doubles easily. Broil the tomatoes in two batches if doubling the recipe. Store the cooled soup in airtight containers or zip-top plastic freezer bags in the refrigerator for up to 4 days, or in the freezer for up to 3 months.

If you love Korean food, you'll adore this quick soup full of napa cabbage kimchi, soft tofu, and fragrant ginger. I sauté bacon with the onions to make the soup more substantial and add umami, but the recipe can be made vegan by omitting the bacon and using a light vegetable broth in lieu of chicken broth.

The slightly sweet egg breads on page 162 are the perfect foil for this spicy Korean soup.

SERVES

4 TO 6

ACTIVE TIME

20 MINUTES

TOTAL TIME

35 MINUTES

Korean Kimchi and Tofu Soup

PAIR WITH

Korean Egg Breads (PAGE 162)

1 Tbsp safflower oil
3 strips thick-cut pepper bacon, chopped
1 medium yellow onion, finely chopped
4 medium garlic cloves, minced
1 Tbsp minced fresh ginger
4 cups [960 ml] vegetable or chicken broth (see page 17)
1½ cups [340 g] chopped napa cabbage kimchi with juice
1 medium zucchini, quartered lengthwise and chopped
2 Tbsp soy sauce or tamari, plus more as needed
2 tsp sugar
1 to 2 Tbsp Sriracha (optional)
1½ cups [340 g] soft tofu, drained
1 tsp toasted sesame oil
4 green onions, thinly sliced

1. Heat the safflower oil in a large soup pot or Dutch oven over medium heat. Add the bacon and cook, stirring frequently, until crisped and browned, about 4 minutes. Remove all but 1 Tbsp of the bacon drippings from the pot; leave the bacon in the pot. Increase the heat to medium-high, add the yellow onion, and sauté until tender, about 4 minutes. Add the garlic and ginger and sauté until fragrant, 45 seconds.

2. Add the vegetable broth, kimchi and juice, zucchini, soy sauce, and sugar to the pot. Cover, reduce the heat to low, and simmer until the zucchini is just tender, about 10 minutes. Taste the soup, and if you prefer it spicier, add the Sriracha. Break up the tofu with a soupspoon into bite-size chunks and add them to the pot. Simmer the soup gently until the tofu is heated through, about 5 minutes.

3. Remove the soup from the heat, add the sesame oil, and season with additional soy sauce, if desired. Ladle the soup into soup bowls and sprinkle with the green onions. Serve immediately.

GET AHEAD: Store the soup in an airtight container in the refrigerator for up to 4 days. It will become spicier with time, so add additional broth, if necessary, to adjust. This soup does not freeze well.

SERVES

4 TO 6

ACTIVE TIME

15
MINUTES

TOTAL TIME

50
MINUTES

This soup gets its soothing creaminess from an unlikely ingredient—oatmeal. The whole grain disintegrates when simmered and blends into the broccoli and broth mixture seamlessly, without adding fat like cream does. This soup is blended to make the soup fairly smooth; skip this step if you prefer chunky soup or are short on time.

For full-on cheesy satisfaction, I pair this soup with toasted slabs of day-old Beer and Cheddar Bread (page 157).

Lighter Broccoli and Cheese Soup

PAIR WITH

Beer and Cheddar Bread (PAGE 157)

1½ cups [120 g] grated sharp
   Cheddar cheese
1 Tbsp cornstarch
1½ lb [680 g] broccoli crowns,
   stems sliced and florets cut
   into 2-in [5-cm] pieces
2 Tbsp extra-virgin olive oil
1 medium yellow onion, finely chopped
2 medium garlic cloves, minced
½ cup [120 ml] dry white wine
4 cups [960 ml] vegetable or
   chicken broth (see page 17)
1½ cups [360 ml] milk
½ cup [50 g] instant rolled oats
½ tsp ground turmeric
1 Tbsp freshly squeezed lemon juice
1 Tbsp Dijon mustard
½ tsp freshly grated nutmeg
Pinch of cayenne pepper
Sea salt
Freshly ground black pepper

1. Toss the cheese and cornstarch together in a medium bowl and set aside at room temperature; the cheese will melt more evenly if it is slightly warm. Place the broccoli in a food processor and pulse until very finely chopped. (Alternatively, finely chop the broccoli with a chef's knife.)

2. Heat the olive oil in a large soup pot or Dutch oven over medium heat. Add the onion and sauté until translucent, about 5 minutes. Add the garlic and cook, stirring constantly, until fragrant, about 45 seconds. Add the wine, increase the heat to medium-high, and cook until the wine has reduced by half, about 1 minute.

3. Add the broccoli, broth, milk, oats, and turmeric to the pot. Cover and bring to a simmer over medium-high heat. Reduce the heat to low and simmer, stirring frequently, until the broccoli and oats are tender, about 20 minutes.

4. Remove the pot from the heat and add the lemon juice, mustard, and nutmeg. Blend the soup in the pot with an immersion blender until smooth, or in batches in the food processor that you used to chop the broccoli. Return the soup to the pot, place over low heat, and add the cheese and cornstarch mixture all at once. Stir the soup with a wooden spoon a few times in a zigzag pattern until the cheese has melted. Add the cayenne and season with salt and pepper.

5. Ladle the soup into bowls, and serve immediately.

GET AHEAD: You can save time by purchasing precut broccoli florets in the produce department of most grocery stores. Pulse the florets in a food processor as directed.

The cooled soup can be stored in airtight containers or zip-top plastic freezer bags in the refrigerator for up to 4 days, or in the freezer for up to 3 months. Defrost in the refrigerator for 24 hours and reheat gently over low heat to prevent the cheese from curdling.

SERVES

4 TO 6

ACTIVE TIME

15

MINUTES

TOTAL TIME

35

MINUTES

If I had to pick a favorite soup, one that makes me happy about the relentless rain and the bone-soaking chill of nights in Oregon, this soup would be it. I love roasted brassicas (the botanical family that includes broccoli, cauliflower, and cabbage) of any kind—dry heat has a way of making them nutty and addictively savory. I add paprika and dill, the flavors of my Polish grandmother's cooking, and finish the soup with a big dollop of sour cream.

Roasted Cauliflower and Paprika Soup

PAIR WITH

Everything Rye Muffins (PAGE 170)

One 12-oz[340-g] head cauliflower, cored and cut into 1-in [2.5-cm] florets

4 medium garlic cloves, unpeeled

3 Tbsp extra-virgin olive oil

Sea salt

Freshly ground black pepper

1 medium yellow onion, chopped

1 large carrot, peeled and thinly sliced

½ cup [120 ml] dry white wine

6 cups [1.5 L] vegetable or chicken broth (see page 17)

4 oz [115 g] red potatoes (2 medium), cut into bite-size pieces

1 Tbsp plus 1 tsp sweet paprika, plus more for garnish

1 bay leaf

5 Tbsp [10 g] chopped fresh dill

1½ Tbsp freshly squeezed lemon juice

¾ cup [180 g] sour cream or plain yogurt

1. Preheat the oven to 425°F [220°C]. Line two baking sheets with parchment paper.

2. In a large bowl, toss the cauliflower and garlic with 2 Tbsp of the olive oil. Divide the florets between the prepared baking sheets, arrange in even layers, and season liberally with salt and pepper. Roast, stirring once, until the cauliflower is tender and lightly browned, about 25 minutes.

3. While the cauliflower is roasting, start the soup. Heat the remaining 1 tablespoon of oil in a large soup pot or Dutch oven over medium heat. Add the onion and carrot and sauté until they begin to brown, about 5 minutes. Immediately add the wine and cook until it has nearly evaporated, about 30 seconds. Add the broth, potatoes, paprika, and bay leaf. Cover and bring to a simmer. Reduce the heat to low and continue simmering.

4. When the roasted cauliflower is tender and lightly browned, add to the soup. Discard the garlic skins, chop the cloves (they will be very soft and sticky), and add them to the soup as well. Simmer the soup, uncovered, stirring occasionally, until the potatoes are fall-apart tender, about 10 minutes. Add 3 Tbsp of the dill and the lemon juice and season with salt and pepper.

5. Ladle the soup into bowls and garnish each one with a generous dollop of sour cream, a few pinches of paprika, and some of the remaining 2 Tbsp of dill.

GET AHEAD: The roasted cauliflower can be stored in an airtight container in the refrigerator for up to 3 days; I often make an extra baking sheet of cauliflower when roasting other vegetables and make this soup a few days later.

The cooled soup (without the sour cream topping or garnishes) can be stored in airtight containers or zip-top plastic freezer bags in the refrigerator for up to 4 days, or in the freezer for up to 3 months. Defrost frozen soup overnight in the refrigerator. Garnish the reheated soup as directed.

SERVES

4 TO 6

ACTIVE TIME

15
MINUTES

TOTAL TIME

35
MINUTES

There are two ways to approach this ode to autumn soup: either peel and cut up a winter squash of your choice (see Get Ahead on page 70), or take a shortcut and use precut butternut squash from the grocery store (look for it in the produce department). Instead of the usual curry powder found in most squash soup recipes, I mix a variety of spices and use the flavorful combo as a spice rub for the squash. You can make this soup vegan by using vegetable broth and garnishing the soup with some chopped smoked almonds.

The breadsticks on page 144 are great for dipping, but I also find that the slightly smoky flavor of green onion pancakes (page 139) plays well with the roasted spices and smoked bacon in this soup.

Spice-Roasted Butternut Squash Soup with Bacon Crumbles

PAIR WITH

Thin and Crispy Breadsticks (PAGE 144)
Flaky Green Onion Pancakes (PAGE 139)

3 medium garlic cloves
1¼ tsp coriander seeds
¾ tsp fennel seeds
8 black peppercorns
¾ tsp sea salt
1 pinch red chile flakes
4 Tbsp [60 ml] extra-virgin olive oil
3 lb [1.4 kg] peeled butternut or
    other winter squash, cut into
    1-in [2.5-cm] chunks
1 medium yellow onion, chopped
1 large carrot, peeled and
    finely chopped
½ cup [120 ml] dry white wine
6 cups [1.4 L] vegetable or
    chicken broth (see page 17)
Sea salt
Freshly ground black pepper
5 strips thick-cut bacon, cooked
    and crumbled
¼ cup [7 g] thinly sliced fresh chives

1. Preheat the oven to 425°F [220°C]. Line two rimmed baking sheets with parchment paper.

2. Combine the garlic, coriander seeds, fennel seeds, peppercorns, salt, and red chile flakes in a mortar and pound with the pestle until the mixture is a fine paste. (Alternatively, mince the garlic and grind the coriander seeds, fennel seeds, peppercorns, and salt in a spice grinder. Combine the spices with the garlic and add the red chile flakes.) Add 3 Tbsp of the olive oil and stir to combine.

3. In a large bowl, toss the squash with the spice and olive oil mixture. Divide the squash between the prepared baking sheets and spread out in even layers. Roast, stirring once, until the squash is tender and browned, about 25 minutes.

CONTINUED

4. Meanwhile, heat the remaining 1 Tbsp of olive oil in a large soup pot or Dutch oven over medium heat. Add the onion and carrot and sauté until golden brown, about 8 minutes. Add the wine and cook, scraping up the browned bits, until the wine has nearly evaporated, about 1 minute.

5. Add the broth to the pot, cover, and bring to a simmer. Reduce the heat to low and simmer while the squash roasts. When the squash is done, add it to the soup, scraping up and adding any spice mixture stuck to the baking sheets as well. Increase the heat to medium, cover, and simmer for 5 minutes.

6. Remove the soup from the heat and blend in the pot with an immersion blender or in batches in a blender, with the lid slightly ajar, until smooth. Return the soup to the pot and warm over low heat until very hot, about 2 minutes. Season with salt and pepper.

7. Ladle the soup into bowls and garnish with the bacon and chives. Serve immediately.

GET AHEAD: This soup freezes well and doubles easily, but you'll need to roast the squash in batches so it roasts evenly. Crowded squash won't brown.

Refrigerate the cooled soup in airtight containers or zip-top plastic freezer bags, without the bacon or chives, for up to 4 days, or freeze for up to 3 months.

I fell for this soothing Cantonese soup years ago at an upscale restaurant in Chinatown in San Francisco. When I was seated, the waiter presented me with the customary cup of soup and a menu. I was relieved to discover that instead of egg drop soup, he had brought me winter melon soup—rich chicken broth with chunks of silky, almost translucent winter melon floating in it. Though the winter melon didn't have much flavor of its own, it absorbed the flavor of the rich broth and had a soft, soothing texture, which I've come to crave on cold winter nights.

Look for winter melon at Asian markets, where the large, light green melons are often broken down and sold in manageable chunks. They are labeled tung gwa *or* dong gua *in Chinese markets and* bí đao *in Vietnamese shops. If you can't find winter melon, substitute peeled and cored chayote squash.*

SERVES

4 TO 6

ACTIVE TIME

20

MINUTES

TOTAL TIME

40

MINUTES

Winter Melon Soup with Smoky Ham

PAIR WITH

Flaky Green Onion Pancakes (PAGE 139)

4 dried shiitake mushrooms

1½ cups [360 ml] boiling water

1½ lb [680 g] winter melon or chayote squash, peeled, seeded, and cut into ½-in [12-mm] chunks

6 cups [1.4 L] vegetable or chicken broth (see page 17)

½ cup [45 g] canned bamboo shoots, cut into thin matchsticks

3 oz [85 g] smoked Canadian bacon, cut into matchsticks 2 in [5 cm] long

1 Tbsp plus 1 tsp minced fresh ginger

2 tsp sugar

2 tsp cornstarch

⅛ tsp ground white pepper

Soy sauce, for seasoning

2 medium green onions, thinly sliced

1. In a small bowl, combine the mushrooms with the boiling water. Place a smaller bowl on top of the mushrooms to keep them entirely submerged, and soak until they are soft, about 20 minutes. Drain the mushrooms, discard the stems, and thinly slice the caps.

2. While the mushrooms soak, combine the winter melon, broth, bamboo shoots, Canadian bacon, ginger, and sugar in a large soup pot or Dutch oven and bring to a simmer over medium-high heat. Cover, reduce the heat to medium-low, and simmer until the winter melon is nearly translucent and feels tender when pierced with a fork, about 20 minutes.

3. In a small bowl, combine the cornstarch with 1 Tbsp cold water. Add the mixture to the soup along with the sliced mushroom caps and the white pepper. Simmer until thickened slightly, about 1 minute. Season with soy sauce.

4. Ladle the soup into soup bowls and garnish with the green onions. Serve immediately.

GET AHEAD: You can keep the mushrooms in their soaking liquid in the refrigerator for up to 1 week. The cooled soup can be kept in airtight containers in the refrigerator for up to 4 days. This soup does not freeze well.

Called sambar *in southern India, this vegan lentil and vegetable stew is often served as a breakfast dish with spongy steamed breads, called* idli. *Sambar is traditionally made with split yellow peas, but I substitute red lentils because they cook in half the time and taste equally lovely. The pleasantly sweet-sour note of this soup comes from packaged tamarind purée or paste (look for nuoc me chua or Vietnamese "sour soup base mix" in Asian markets). If you have thick, molasses-like Indian tamarind concentrate on hand, reduce the amount to 1 tsp and dilute it in 1 Tbsp of warm water. I use slender Japanese eggplant, carrot, and green beans in this soup, but the recipe is very adaptable. Go shopping in your vegetable keeper and use what you have on hand—cauliflower, cabbage, red bell pepper, parsnips, and zucchini are all good additions.*

SERVES

6

ACTIVE TIME

15

MINUTES

TOTAL TIME

40

MINUTES

South Indian Sambar

PAIR WITH

Indian Steamed Rice Cakes (PAGE 159)

1 cup [210 g] red lentils,
　　picked over and rinsed
1½ tsp curry powder
1 tsp ground coriander
Sea salt
1 Japanese eggplant, cut into
　　½-in [12-mm] chunks
1 large carrot, peeled and chopped
4 oz [115 g] green beans, trimmed
　　and cut into bite-size pieces
1 medium shallot, thinly sliced
1 serrano chile, chopped
2 Tbsp safflower or coconut oil
1½ tsp brown mustard seeds
10 curry leaves (optional)
1 Tbsp minced fresh ginger
2 medium garlic cloves, minced
1 medium plum tomato, chopped
1 Tbsp tamarind purée or paste
　　(see headnote)
Freshly ground black pepper

1. Combine the lentils, curry powder, coriander, 1½ tsp salt, and 5½ cups [1.3 L] hot water in a large soup pot or Dutch oven. Bring to a boil over medium-high heat, stirring frequently to make sure the lentils don't stick to the bottom of the pot. Add the eggplant, carrot, green beans, shallot, and serrano chile and reduce the heat to low. Cover and simmer until the vegetables and lentils are very tender, about 20 minutes.

2. Heat the safflower oil in a small sauté pan over medium heat. Add the mustard seeds and curry leaves (if using) and cook until the seeds begin to pop, about 20 seconds. Add the ginger and garlic and sauté until fragrant but not browned, about 45 seconds. Scrape the seasonings into the pot (careful, the oil will sputter). Add the tomato and tamarind to the pot, stir, and simmer for 5 minutes. Season with salt and pepper.

3. Ladle the soup into bowls and serve immediately.

GET AHEAD: This soup tastes even better the second or third day (though it does get spicier and thicker as it rests). When reheating, add additional water to restore the original soupy consistency and season with salt. You can also freeze the cooled soup in airtight containers or zip-top plastic freezer bags for up to 3 months.

SERVES

4 TO 6

ACTIVE TIME

25 MINUTES

TOTAL TIME

45 MINUTES

Cream, potatoes, and broth balance the spiciness of the glossy, dark green poblanos in this soup, but keep in mind that heat varies greatly from chile to chile. I recommend tasting each roasted chile as you peel it, and adjusting accordingly; you may not want to use them all if you've got an extra-spicy batch. Extra roasted poblanos can be stored in an airtight container in the refrigerator for up to 1 week or in the freezer for up to 1 month. Try them on nachos or as a topping for burgers!

The sweetness of the apple and cheddar muffins on page 171 or the corn and maple skillet bread on page 152 will counter the spiciness of this chowder well.

Spicy Roasted Poblano and Potato Chowder

PAIR WITH

Quinoa, Apple, and Cheddar Muffins (PAGE 171)
Blue Corn and Maple Skillet Bread (PAGE 152)

3 medium poblano chiles
2 Tbsp unsalted butter
1 large yellow onion, finely chopped
2 celery stalks, thinly sliced
4 medium garlic cloves, minced
1 Tbsp chopped fresh oregano or
   1 tsp dried Mexican oregano
4 cups [960 ml] vegetable or
   chicken broth (see page 17)
2 lb [910 g] baking potatoes
   (about 3 medium),
   peeled and thinly sliced
3 Tbsp masa harina or fine cornmeal
1 cup [240 ml] heavy cream
Sea salt
Freshly ground black pepper
1 cup [140 g] grated
   Monterey Jack cheese

1. Adjust the oven rack so that it is 6 in [15 cm] below the heating element, and preheat the broiler.

2. Place the poblanos on a small, heavy baking sheet. Broil, turning with tongs once, until the skins are blackened all over, 10 to 12 minutes.

3. Melt the butter in a large soup pot or Dutch oven over medium heat. Add the onion and celery and sauté until the onion is translucent, about 4 minutes. Add the garlic and oregano and sauté until fragrant, about 45 seconds. Add the broth and potatoes, cover, and bring to a simmer. Reduce the heat to low and continue simmering while you prep the chiles.

4. Remove and discard the stems and seeds from the chiles. Scrape off and discard the blackened skins from the chiles with a butter knife. (It's fine if there are a few blackened bits left; just do your best to get most of them off.) Chop the chiles and add them to the soup pot. Cover and simmer over low heat, stirring frequently, until the potatoes are fall-apart tender, about 15 minutes. (The potatoes will start out in whole pieces, but they will break up as they cook.)

5. Place the masa in a medium bowl and gradually whisk in the cream. Add the mixture to the soup and cook, uncovered, until thickened and bubbly, about 5 minutes. Season with salt and pepper.

6. Ladle the soup into bowls and sprinkle with the grated cheese. Serve immediately.

GET AHEAD: Roasting and peeling poblano chiles requires a few minutes; you can opt for jarred roasted poblanos to save time.

The cooled soup (without cheese) can be stored in airtight containers or zip-top plastic freezer bags in the refrigerator for up to 4 days, or in the freezer for up to 3 months. Defrost overnight in the refrigerator and reheat very gently. (See the Get Ahead note on page 85 about the texture of frozen and reheated chowder.)

Bean and Grain Soups

This spicy, thick lentil soup acquires its complex flavor from berbere, an East African spice blend that includes coriander, fenugreek, dried chiles, and fried shallots. You can find packaged berbere spice at international markets and online, but it's fun and easy to make it yourself, so I've included directions for making it here. You will have enough for two batches of soup. Or try the leftover mixture on popcorn, fried eggs, or as a rub for grilled meats!

Serve the soup with the teff pancakes on page 145, tearing off pieces of the spongy, crêpe-like breads with your hands and using them to scoop up the thick soup.

Spicy Ethiopian Red Lentil Soup

PAIR WITH

Savory Teff Pancakes (PAGE 145)

BERBERE SPICE BLEND

2 tsp coriander seeds
1 tsp fenugreek seeds
½ tsp black peppercorns
2 green cardamom pods
3 whole cloves
½ cup [30 g] dried fried shallots
   (see Flavor Toolbox, page 14)
3 to 6 dried red chiles de árbol,
   stemmed, seeded, and broken up
3 Tbsp sweet paprika
1½ tsp sea salt
½ tsp ground allspice
½ tsp ground cinnamon
½ tsp ground ginger
½ tsp ground nutmeg

RED LENTIL SOUP

2 Tbsp extra-virgin olive oil
1 large yellow onion, finely chopped
3 medium Anaheim chiles,
   seeded and chopped
2 Tbsp minced fresh ginger
3 medium garlic cloves, minced
2 Tbsp tomato paste
3 cups [630 g] red lentils,
   picked over and rinsed
Sea salt
Freshly ground black pepper
3 Tbsp unsalted butter or coconut oil

CONTINUED

1. **TO MAKE THE SPICE BLEND:** Toast the coriander seeds, fenugreek seeds, peppercorns, cardamom pods, and cloves in a small, dry saucepan over medium heat, stirring constantly until fragrant, about 3 minutes. Let the toasted spices cool slightly and transfer them to a spice grinder along with the fried shallots and dried chiles. Grind the spices until the mixture is finely ground, about 1 minute. (Alternatively, grind the spices with a mortar and pestle.) Transfer the mixture to a small bowl and add the paprika, salt, allspice, cinnamon, ginger, and nutmeg.

2. **TO MAKE THE SOUP:** Heat the oil in a large soup pot or Dutch oven over medium heat. Add the onion and Anaheim chiles and sauté, stirring frequently, until the onion is golden brown, about 8 minutes. Add the ginger and garlic and sauté until fragrant, about 1 minute. Add 3½ Tbsp of the *berbere* and the tomato paste and stir to combine.

3. Add the lentils, 8 cups [2 L] cold water, and 1 tsp salt. Cover and bring to a simmer. Reduce the heat to low and simmer, stirring frequently to make sure the lentils don't stick to the bottom of the pot, until the lentils are fall-apart tender, 30 minutes. Season with salt and pepper.

4. Ladle the soup into bowls, top each with a dab of butter, and sprinkle with a generous pinch of *berbere*. Serve immediately.

GET AHEAD: Store the cooled soup in airtight containers or zip-top plastic freezer bags in the refrigerator for up to 4 days, or in the freezer for up to 3 months. Reheat gently over low heat, adding a bit of water if needed to adjust the consistency. Add a squeeze of lemon juice and additional *berbere*, if necessary, to wake up the flavors.

Store the spice blend in an airtight container at room temperature for up to 6 months.

SERVES

4 TO 6

ACTIVE TIME

15

MINUTES

TOTAL TIME

45

MINUTES

This is an old-school recipe I learned to make in the early '90s, while I was working in a gourmet deli. It was, hands down, our best seller, and it's still a favorite with my family. Don't be tempted to skip the dry sherry and sherry vinegar here; they add a bright, acidic tang, which amplifies all the flavors in this soup. The red pepper cream swirl on top boosts the color of the soup and spikes it with a beautifully smoky flavor.

Black Bean Soup with Roasted Red Pepper Cream

PAIR WITH

Brazilian Tapioca and Cheese Rolls (PAGE 165)
Spinach and Sun-Dried Tomato Scones (PAGE 154)

BLACK BEAN SOUP

3 Tbsp extra-virgin olive oil
1 large yellow onion, chopped
1 medium green bell pepper, seeded and chopped
3 medium garlic cloves, minced
1 Tbsp chopped fresh thyme
1 tsp ground cumin
1 tsp ground coriander
4½ cups [800 g] cooked black beans (see page 19), or three 15-oz [425-g] cans black beans, rinsed and drained
4 cups [960 ml] chicken or vegetable broth (see page 17)
1 bay leaf

ROASTED RED PEPPER CREAM

½ cup [120 ml] heavy cream
½ cup [160 g] jarred roasted red peppers
1½ tsp freshly squeezed lemon juice
½ tsp sea salt
¼ tsp smoked paprika
⅛ tsp cayenne pepper

¼ cup [60 ml] dry sherry
1 Tbsp Spanish sherry vinegar
Sea salt
Freshly ground black pepper

1. **TO MAKE THE SOUP:** Heat the oil in a large soup pot or Dutch oven over medium heat. Add the onion and bell pepper and sauté until they begin to brown, about 8 minutes. Add the garlic, thyme, cumin, and coriander and cook, stirring constantly, until fragrant, about 45 seconds. Add the beans, broth, and bay leaf. Cover and bring to a simmer. Reduce the heat to low and simmer, stirring occasionally, for 20 minutes.

2. **TO MAKE THE RED PEPPER CREAM:** Place the cream, red peppers, lemon juice, salt, paprika, and cayenne pepper in a blender and blend until smooth. Pour the mixture into a bowl and set aside while you finish the soup.

3. Remove the bay leaf from the soup and purée in the pot with an immersion blender, or in batches in a clean blender with the lid slightly ajar, until almost smooth. (I like to leave some of the beans unblended, but you can blend all the way to smooth, if you like.) Return the soup to the pot, add the sherry and sherry vinegar, and heat over low heat for 5 minutes. Season with salt and pepper.

4. Ladle the soup into bowls, spoon some of the red pepper cream on top, and swirl. Serve immediately.

GET AHEAD: The soup and Roasted Red Pepper Cream can be stored in the refrigerator in separate airtight containers for up to 4 days. The soup (without the red pepper cream) freezes well in airtight containers or zip-top plastic freezer bags for up to 3 months. Reheat gently over low heat until hot.

SERVES

4 TO **6**

ACTIVE TIME

15

MINUTES

TOTAL TIME

40

MINUTES

This soup is my approximation of a memorable white bean soup I had in a small trattoria in the remote Tuscan hill town of Volterra. It was creamy and rich, with a depth of flavor that belied its simple description as "white bean soup." I begged the proprietress in broken Italian for the secret to the soup and was shocked to learn that she sautéed a few anchovies with the vegetables. The anchovies add richness and umami, but there's no overt fishiness in the flavor of the soup. I garnish the soup with a spoonful of gremolata (finely chopped parsley, lemon zest, and garlic) mixed with peppery Tuscan olive oil. The result is a soup that's filling but light, and incredibly simple to make.

Serve this soup with the Tuscan-inspired, garlicky focaccia on page 142 to get the last drops from the bottom of the bowl.

Creamy Cannellini Bean Soup with Gremolata

PAIR WITH

Roasted Garlic Focaccia (PAGE 142)

4 Tbsp [60 ml] extra-virgin olive oil, preferably Tuscan
1 medium yellow onion, finely chopped
1 large carrot, peeled and finely chopped
1 celery stalk, finely chopped
1 Tbsp plus 1 tsp chopped fresh sage
2 medium oil-packed anchovies
½ cup [120 ml] dry white wine
4 cups [960 ml] chicken or vegetable broth (see page 17)
4½ cups [675 g] cooked cannellini beans (see page 19), or three 15-oz [425-g] cans cannellini beans, rinsed and drained
1 bay leaf
¼ cup [7 g] fresh Italian parsley leaves
2½ tsp finely grated lemon zest
1 small garlic clove, peeled (remove the green sprout in the center, if present)

Sea salt
Freshly ground black pepper

1. In a large soup pot or Dutch oven, heat 2 Tbsp of the olive oil over medium-high heat. Add the onion, carrot, celery, sage, and anchovies and cook, stirring occasionally, until the onion is translucent, about 4 minutes. Add the wine and cook, scraping up browned bits on the bottom of the pan, until the wine has nearly evaporated, about 1 minute.

2. Add 1 cup [240 ml] hot water, the chicken broth, beans, and bay leaf. Cover and bring to a simmer over medium-high heat. Reduce the heat to medium-low and simmer, stirring occasionally, until the vegetables are very tender, about 20 minutes.

56

3. On a cutting board, mound the parsley, lemon zest, and garlic. Sprinkle with a little salt and chop very finely until the mixture is a bit wet looking. Transfer to a small bowl, add the remaining 2 Tbsp olive oil, and stir to combine the gremolata.

4. Remove the bay leaf and blend the soup with an immersion blender in the pot, or in batches in a blender with the lid slightly ajar, until smooth. Return the soup to the pot and reheat over medium-low heat until very hot, about 2 minutes. Season with salt and pepper.

5. Ladle the soup into soup bowls and drizzle each with the parsley-oil mixture. Serve immediately.

GET AHEAD: Store the cooled soup in airtight containers or zip-top plastic freezer bags in the refrigerator for up to 4 days, or in the freezer for up to 3 months. The gremolata is best made immediately before serving.

SERVES

4 TO 6

ACTIVE TIME

15
MINUTES

TOTAL TIME

45
MINUTES

I had this somewhat unlikely-sounding soup, called jota in Friulian dialect, in Trieste, in the far northeastern part of Italy. The city has alternately been part of Slovenia or Italy for centuries (it's a border town), thus this very Slavic-looking soup of sauerkraut, potatoes, and beans. I know it sounds weird, but once you try it, you'll be hooked. Not overtly sauerkraut-y and perfectly hearty without being heavy, it's just the thing for a snowy evening. The soup can be made vegan by omitting the pancetta and using vegetable broth.

This soup is best with either an eastern European bread or muffin (see page 170) or an Italian bread or roll (see page 163).

Friulian Bean and Sauerkraut Soup

PAIR WITH

Everything Rye Muffins (PAGE 170)
Olive and Prosciutto Rolls (PAGE 163)

2 Tbsp extra-virgin olive oil, plus more for garnish

3 oz [85 g] pancetta, chopped (buy a thick slab from the butcher and chop it yourself for the best texture)

1 large yellow onion, chopped

2 medium garlic cloves, minced

1 tsp ground cumin

6 whole juniper berries, coarsely crushed with the bottom of a heavy pan

½ cup [120 ml] dry white wine

6 cups [1.4 L] chicken or vegetable broth (see page 17)

3 cups [500 g] cooked cranberry or borlotti beans (see page 19), or two 15-oz [425-g] cans cranberry or borlotti beans, rinsed and drained

1 lb [455 g] sauerkraut, drained but not rinsed

1 lb [455 g] Yukon Gold potatoes (about 3 medium), peeled and cut into bite-size chunks

1 bay leaf

1 Tbsp apple cider vinegar

Sea salt

Freshly ground black pepper

¼ cup [7 g] chopped fresh Italian parsley, for garnish

CONTINUED

1. Heat the oil in a large soup pot or Dutch oven over medium-high heat. Add the pancetta and onion and sauté, stirring frequently, until the onion begins to brown, about 7 minutes. Add the garlic, cumin, and juniper berries and sauté until fragrant, about 1 minute. Add the wine and cook, scraping up browned bits on the bottom of the pot, until the wine has nearly evaporated, about 1 minute.

2. Add the chicken broth, beans, sauerkraut, potatoes, and bay leaf to the pot. Cover and bring to a simmer. Reduce the heat to medium-low and simmer, stirring frequently (especially on the bottom of the pot to make sure the potatoes aren't sticking) until the potatoes are tender and the flavors have melded, about 20 minutes. Discard the bay leaf. Add the vinegar and season with salt and pepper.

3. Ladle the soup into bowls, sprinkle each one with parsley, and drizzle with olive oil. Serve immediately.

GET AHEAD: Store in airtight containers in the refrigerator for up to 4 days. The soup will thicken with time, which is actually a nice thing, I think. By day four, I treat the leftovers more like the French sauerkraut casserole *choucroute garni*, perhaps adding a grilled kielbasa to the mix to change things up. This soup does not freeze particularly well as it causes the sauerkraut to break up too much.

A Cajun "holy trinity" of onions, celery, and bell pepper forms the backbone of this zesty soup. Red beans, long-grain rice, fresh Cajun sausage, and a swig of lager make it the ideal supper for Mardi Gras, or any Tuesday for that matter.

SERVES

4 TO 6

ACTIVE TIME

20 MINUTES

TOTAL TIME

50 MINUTES

Cajun Red Beans and Rice Soup

PAIR WITH

Blue Corn and Maple Skillet Bread (PAGE 152)
Gluten-Free Corn Muffins (PAGE 167)

1¼ lb [570 g] chicken or fresh pork Cajun sausages, casings discarded
1 Tbsp extra-virgin olive oil
1 medium yellow onion, chopped
1 medium green bell pepper, seeded and chopped
2 celery stalks, thinly sliced
1 Tbsp chopped fresh thyme
3 medium garlic cloves, minced
1 tsp Cajun seasoning
1 cup [240 ml] lager beer
2 cups [480 ml] chicken broth (see page 17)
One 28-oz [800-g] can diced tomatoes with juice
1½ cups [255 g] cooked small red beans (see page 19), or one 15-oz [425-g] can red beans, rinsed and drained
½ cup [100 g] long-grain rice
2 bay leaves
Sea salt
Freshly ground black pepper
Hot sauce, for serving

1. Preheat the oven to 400°F [200°C]. Line a small baking sheet with parchment paper.

2. Pinch off bite-size dabs of the sausage meat and place on the baking sheet. Bake until the meat is no longer pink in the center, about 10 minutes.

3. While the sausage cooks, heat the olive oil in a large soup pot or Dutch oven over medium-high heat. Add the onion, bell pepper, celery, and thyme and sauté until the onion is translucent, about 5 minutes. Add the garlic and Cajun seasoning and cook until fragrant, about 45 seconds.

4. Add the beer to the pot and cook, scraping up the browned bits on the bottom of the pot, until the beer has reduced by half, about 2 minutes. Add the chicken broth, tomatoes, beans, rice, and bay leaves. Cover the pot and bring to a simmer.

5. With a slotted spoon, transfer the sausage to the pot, discarding the drippings. Reduce the heat to low and simmer gently, stirring occasionally, until the rice is just tender, 20 minutes. Season with salt and pepper.

6. Ladle the soup into bowls. Serve immediately, and pass the hot sauce at the table.

GET AHEAD: The flavor of this soup improves with time. Store in airtight containers or zip-top plastic freezer bags in the refrigerator for up to 4 days. The rice will absorb a lot of the liquid, so add additional broth when reheating to adjust the consistency, if desired. This soup does not freeze well.

There are versions of this creamy yogurt and lentil soup all over the eastern Mediterranean. In this recipe, the onions, broth, and bulgur (dried cracked wheat kernels) simmer together and then are enriched with yogurt, egg, and a little corn-starch, to prevent the soup from curdling. A helping of the spice-simmered French green lentils (lentilles du Puy) is spooned into each bowl of soup, and it is finished with fresh mint sizzled in brown butter. It tastes like it came from a fancy rooftop restaurant in Tel Aviv, but in reality it's one of the easiest recipes in this book. To make the dish gluten-free, substitute 1 cup [180 g] cooked rice for the bulgur.

I like to plunk a batch of flatbreads dusted with dukkah topping (see page 135) in the center of the table and invite everyone to tear off pieces with their hands to dip in the soup. It turns a weeknight meal into a communal feast!

Persian Yogurt, Lentil, and Bulgur Soup with Browned Herb Butter

PAIR WITH

Quick Flatbread with Dukkah (PAGE 135)

¾ cup [150 g] French green lentils, picked over and rinsed
4 medium garlic cloves, sliced
1 bay leaf
½ cinnamon stick
Sea salt
5 cups [1.2 L] chicken or vegetable broth (see page 17)
1 medium yellow onion, finely chopped
½ cup [90 g] medium bulgur
1½ Tbsp cornstarch
2 cups [480 g] plain full-fat Greek yogurt
1 large egg
Freshly ground black pepper
5 Tbsp [70 g] unsalted butter
½ cup [15 g] chopped fresh mint
2 Tbsp freshly squeezed lemon juice
Pinch of cayenne pepper

1. In a medium saucepan, combine the lentils with 3 cups [720 ml] water, the garlic, bay leaf, cinnamon stick, and ½ tsp salt and bring to a boil over high heat. Reduce the heat to low, cover, and cook until the lentils are tender, about 20 minutes. (If the lentils are not done, add more water and continue to simmer until they are tender to the bite.) Drain the lentils, discard the cinnamon stick and bay leaf, and set the lentils aside. Wipe out the pan and set it aside.

2. While the lentils simmer, combine the chicken broth, onion, and bulgur in a large soup pot or Dutch oven and bring to a simmer over medium-high heat. Reduce the heat to low and simmer, uncovered, until the onion and bulgur are tender, 10 minutes. Turn off the heat.

3. In a medium bowl, whisk the cornstarch with the yogurt and egg until smooth.

4. Gradually whisk 2 cups [480 ml] of the warm soup into the yogurt mixture. Pour the yogurt mixture back into the soup pot and cook, uncovered, over low heat, stirring occasionally, until the soup just begins to bubble and coats the back of a ladle in a thick layer, about 5 minutes. Season with salt and black pepper.

5. Place the butter in the pan used to cook the lentils and melt over medium heat.

Add 2 Tbsp of the mint and cook, stirring occasionally, until the butter is lightly browned and nutty smelling, about 2 minutes. Remove the pan from the heat and add the lemon juice (careful, it will sputter).

6. Ladle the soup into bowls, spoon some of the lentils into the center of each serving, and top with some of the browned butter mixture and a pinch of cayenne pepper. Garnish with the remaining mint. Serve immediately.

GET AHEAD: The lentils can easily be doubled, so you'll have a stash in the freezer for a future soup or salad. Store the cooled lentils in airtight containers or zip-top plastic freezer bags in the refrigerator for up to 5 days, or in the freezer for up to 3 months. Reheat in the microwave or on the stove top over low heat with a bit of water before serving.

The cooled yogurt-bulgur broth (without lentils or browned butter) can be stored in airtight containers or zip-top plastic freezer bags in the refrigerator for up to 4 days, or in the freezer for up to 3 months. Defrost overnight in the refrigerator before reheating gently until warm to the touch; do not boil. Add the warmed lentils, browned butter, and mint as directed.

A bit reminiscent of old-fashioned mushroom-barley soup, this version gets a modern update with earthy quinoa and wild mushrooms. The protein in the quinoa plus the meatiness of the mushrooms make this hearty soup a satisfying meal; no one will notice that it's vegan.

Many Mushroom and Quinoa Soup

PAIR WITH

Quinoa, Apple, and Cheddar Muffins (PAGE 171)

SERVES

6

ACTIVE TIME

25

MINUTES

TOTAL TIME

45

MINUTES

1 oz [30 g] dried porcini mushrooms
1 cup [240 ml] boiling water
2 Tbsp extra-virgin olive oil
8 oz [230 g] wild or wild-cultivated mushrooms (oyster, cremini, or shiitake), tough stems discarded, caps and tender stems sliced
Sea salt
Freshly ground black pepper
¼ cup [60 ml] dry sherry
1 large yellow onion, chopped
1 medium red bell pepper, seeded and chopped
2 celery stalks, thinly sliced
1 large carrot, peeled and thinly sliced into coins
4 cups [960 ml] mushroom broth
One 14.5-oz [410-g] can fire-roasted diced tomatoes with juice
½ cup [85 g] quinoa, rinsed
1 Tbsp fresh chopped marjoram or oregano, or 2 tsp dried marjoram or oregano
1 Tbsp soy sauce or tamari

1. In a small bowl, combine the dried mushrooms with the boiling water. Place a smaller bowl on top of the mushrooms to keep them entirely submerged and soak until they are soft, about 20 minutes.

2. Meanwhile, heat the oil in a large soup pot or Dutch oven over medium-high heat. Add the wild mushrooms, sprinkle with 1 tsp salt and ¼ tsp pepper, and cook, stirring frequently, until the mushrooms have given off their liquid and are browned, about 4 minutes. Add the sherry and cook until it has evaporated, about 1 minute.

3. Add the onion, bell pepper, celery, and carrot to the pot and sauté until the onion is just tender, about 4 minutes.

4. Remove the porcini mushrooms from their soaking liquid, chop them, and add them to the pot. Pour most of the mushroom soaking liquid into the pot, discarding the grit and the last 1 Tbsp or so of liquid at the bottom of the bowl. Add the mushroom broth, tomatoes and juice, quinoa, and marjoram. Cover and bring to a simmer. Reduce the heat to low and simmer, stirring occasionally, until the quinoa is tender, about 20 minutes. Add the soy sauce and season with salt and pepper.

5. Ladle the soup into bowls and serve immediately.

GET AHEAD: Store in airtight containers or zip-top plastic freezer bags in the refrigerator for up to 4 days, or in the freezer for up to 3 months. Defrost overnight in the refrigerator before reheating it gently. The quinoa will thicken it quite a bit; add additional broth, if necessary, to adjust the consistency.

The formula for minestrone is very adaptable—substitute green beans for the cauliflower, chopped cabbage for the kale, or omit the pancetta and cheese to make the soup vegan. Farro is an ancient whole grain related to wheat. The nutty kernels pop when you chew them, adding a nice textural contrast to the tender vegetables. If you're not a fan of chewy grains in soup, look for quick-cooking semi-pearled farro grains at grocery stores and online.

The focaccia on page 142 and the rolls on page 163 both act as ideal sponges for soaking up this brothy soup.

Farro Minestrone

PAIR WITH

Roasted Garlic Focaccia (PAGE 142)

Olive and Prosciutto Rolls (PAGE 163)

2 Tbsp extra-virgin olive oil

1½ oz [40 g] pancetta or bacon, finely chopped (optional)

1 large yellow onion, finely chopped

1 large carrot, peeled and finely chopped

1 medium parsnip, peeled and finely chopped

2 celery stalks, thinly sliced

2 tsp chopped fresh rosemary

2 medium garlic cloves, minced

½ cup [120 ml] dry white wine

6 cups [1.4 L] vegetable or chicken broth (see page 17)

One 14½-oz [410-g] can diced tomatoes with Italian herbs, with juice

1 cup [180 g] farro

1½ cups [180 g] bite-size cauliflower florets

2 cups [115 g] thinly sliced Lacinato kale (remove center rib before slicing)

One 2-in [5-cm] chunk Parmigiano-Reggiano cheese rind (optional)

1½ cups [265 g] cooked borlotti, cranberry, or cannellini beans (see page 19), or one 14-oz [400-g] can cannellini or bortlotti beans, rinsed and drained

Sea salt

Freshly ground black pepper

1. Heat the olive oil in a large soup pot or Dutch oven over medium-high heat. Add the pancetta (if using) and cook until it begins to brown, about 4 minutes. Add the onion, carrot, parsnip, and celery and cook, stirring frequently, until the onion becomes translucent, about 5 minutes. Add the rosemary and garlic and cook until fragrant, about 45 seconds.

2. Add the wine to the pot and cook, scraping up any browned bits, until the wine has nearly evaporated, about 1 minute. Add the vegetable broth, tomatoes, farro, cauliflower, kale, and cheese rind (if using). Cover and bring to a simmer. Reduce the heat to low and simmer gently, stirring occasionally, until the farro is almost tender, 20 minutes.

3. Add the beans to the pot, cover, and cook until the farro is tender but still has a nice chewiness, about 10 minutes. Discard the cheese rind and season the soup with salt and pepper.

4. Ladle the soup into bowls and serve immediately.

GET AHEAD: The soup tastes even better the next day. Store in airtight containers or zip-top plastic freezer bags in the refrigerator for up to 4 days, or in the freezer for up to 3 months. The grain and beans will absorb a lot of the liquid, so you may need to add broth when reheating to achieve the desired consistency.

SERVES

4 TO 6

ACTIVE TIME

20 MINUTES

TOTAL TIME

45 MINUTES

I love the way the rich, salty pancetta plays against the sweetness of pumpkin in this ode to autumn. The short-grain arborio rice, traditionally used in risotto, makes the soup soothing and filling. For the most delicious results, get an heirloom variety of pumpkin like Long Island Cheese pumpkin, Rouge Vif D'Étampes (aka Cinderella pumpkin), or a Queensland Blue pumpkin from the farmers' market. It takes about 30 minutes to take down a squash and dice it, and a 6-lb [2.7-kg] pumpkin will yield 15 cups [2 kg] of diced pumpkin—enough for three batches of soup. And since winter squash freezes well, a little effort now will pay off later. If you're in a hurry, you can always use prediced packages of butternut squash from the produce department for this recipe.

The fall flavors of this dish are a natural with the toasty sage notes of the bannock bread on page 153 or the potato farls on page 138.

Pumpkin, Pancetta, and Arborio Rice Soup

PAIR WITH

Bannock Bread with Browned Butter and Sage (PAGE 153)
Potato Rosemary Farls (PAGE 138)

1 Tbsp extra-virgin olive oil
3 oz [85 g] finely chopped pancetta
    or thick-cut bacon
1 large leek, white and light green parts
    only, rinsed well and thinly sliced
4 cups [510 g] bite-size pieces
    peeled pumpkin or winter squash
    (see Get Ahead)
2 medium garlic cloves, minced
½ cup [120 ml] dry white wine
4 cups [960 ml] chicken broth
    (see page 17)
½ cup [100 g] arborio rice
One 3-in [7.5-cm] chunk Parmigiano-
    Reggiano cheese rind, plus
    grated Parmigiano-Reggiano
    cheese for serving
1 pinch dried red chile flakes
Sea salt
Freshly ground black pepper

1. Heat the oil in a large soup pot or a Dutch oven over medium-high heat. Add the pancetta and sauté until it has rendered all its fat and begins to brown, about 4 minutes. Add the leek and sauté until tender, about 3 minutes more. Add the pumpkin and garlic and cook, stirring occasionally, until the pumpkin begins to soften a little, another 4 minutes.

2. Add the wine to the pot and cook until nearly evaporated, about 1 minute. Add the chicken broth, 2 cups [480 ml] hot water, the rice, cheese rind, and red chile flakes. Cover and bring to a simmer. Reduce the heat to low and simmer until the squash is tender, about 15 minutes. Discard the cheese rind. If you would like a thicker soup, increase the heat to medium-high and cook, uncovered, for 5 minutes more. Season with salt and pepper.

CONTINUED

3. Ladle the soup into bowls. Serve immediately, with grated Parmigiano-Reggiano on the side.

GET AHEAD: To break down thick-skinned pumpkin or winter squash safely, prick them with a fork and microwave for a few minutes or bake them in a 400°F [200°C] oven for 10 minutes to soften the skin a little. Break off the stem and plunge a sharp chef's knife into the top of the pumpkin, where the stem was. Push downward to the bottom of the pumpkin, and repeat on the opposite side, effectively cleaving the pumpkin in half. With a soup spoon, scrape out and discard the seeds and stringy bits. With a sharp vegetable peeler or a chef's knife, peel off the skins and discard. Chop the pumpkin into pieces—about ¾ in [2 cm] square—and use as directed or freeze in zip-top plastic freezer bags for up to 3 months. The frozen chopped pumpkin can go directly into this recipe from the freezer; it will take an additional 5 minutes of sautéing to warm it.

This is the "pasta fazool" Dean Martin sings about in his goofy hit "That's Amore." Fasul is the Neapolitan pronunciation of fagioli, or beans, and this soup does indeed feature beans and pasta. I've found that adding regular dried pasta to the soup thickens it a bit too much, so I use no-boil lasagna noodle pieces or some of the new "one-pot" pasta shapes that are formulated to be cooked in the sauce, such as Barilla's Pronto elbows or rotini. The result is a hearty but fresh-tasting vegetarian soup that's a perfect Italian trattoria–style meal when paired with the flatbread topped with pecorino cheese on page 135.

SERVES

4 TO 6

ACTIVE TIME

15

MINUTES

TOTAL TIME

40

MINUTES

Broken Pasta and Bean Soup

PAIR WITH

Quick Flatbread with Olive and Pecorino Topping (PAGE 135)

1 Tbsp extra-virgin olive oil,
   plus more for drizzling (optional)
   if not using truffle oil
1 medium yellow onion, finely chopped
2 celery stalks, finely chopped
1 large carrot, peeled and
   finely chopped
1 pt [320 g] cherry tomatoes, halved
2 medium garlic cloves, minced
5½ cups [1.3 L] vegetable, chicken,
   or beef broth (see page 17 or 18)
3 cups [515 g] cooked borlotti or
   cannellini beans (see page 19), or
   two 15-oz [425-g] cans borlotti or
   cannellini beans, rinsed and drained
One 3-in [7.5-cm] chunk Parmigiano-
   Reggiano cheese rind
2 oz [55 g] no-boil lasagna noodles,
   broken into bite-size pieces, or
   ¾ cup [55 g] no-boil short pasta
⅛ tsp red chile flakes
Sea salt
Freshly ground black pepper

White truffle oil, for drizzling
(optional)

1. Heat the olive oil in a large soup pot or Dutch oven over medium heat. Add the onion, celery, and carrot and sauté until the onion is translucent, about 4 minutes. Add the tomatoes and garlic and sauté until the tomatoes begin to collapse, about 4 minutes.

2. Add the vegetable broth, beans, cheese rind, noodles, and red chile flakes to the pot. Cover and bring to a simmer. Reduce the heat to low and simmer gently, stirring occasionally, until the vegetables and pasta are tender, about 15 minutes.

3. Discard the cheese rind and season the soup with salt and pepper. Use a potato masher to mash about half of the beans in the pot to make the soup creamier.

4. Ladle the soup into bowls and top each serving with a drizzle of truffle oil (if using) or olive oil. Serve immediately.

GET AHEAD: The soup is better the next day, but the pasta will begin to absorb the liquid, so you may need to add additional broth and adjust the seasoning when reheating. Store in airtight containers or zip-top plastic freezer bags in the refrigerator for up to 5 days, or in the freezer for up to 3 months. If you freeze the soup, the pasta will soften, but the soup will still be excellent. Defrost in the refrigerator overnight before reheating it gently.

Seafood Soups and Chowders

Seamus Foran, chef of Acadia Bistro in Portland, Oregon, shared this recipe for his intensely corn-flavored soup with me after I raved about it one late-summer evening. The chef's secret for intense corn flavor is to make a quick broth using the cobs. He garnishes the soup with lump crabmeat and crisp bacon, but for a nice vegetarian alternative, you can substitute wild mushrooms, thinly sliced and sautéed in butter until browned and crisp.

The sweetness of the corn in this elegant soup pairs beautifully with the saltiness of the Gruyère in the pastry puffs on page 166.

SERVES

4 TO 6

ACTIVE TIME

20 MINUTES

TOTAL TIME

50 MINUTES

Crab Buttermilk Bisque with Sweet Corn and Bacon

PAIR WITH

Gruyère Cheese Choux Pastry Puffs (PAGE 166)

6 medium ears fresh corn, shucked
8 black peppercorns
2 bay leaves
2 sprigs fresh thyme
2 Tbsp unsalted butter
1 medium yellow onion, finely chopped
Sea salt
¼ tsp cayenne pepper
1 cup [240 ml] buttermilk,
    at room temperature
Freshly ground black pepper
8 oz [230 g] lump crabmeat,
    picked over
4 strips thick-cut bacon,
    cooked and crumbled
18 small baby spinach leaves

1. Shave the corn kernels from the cobs by holding a cob upright on the cutting board with the tapered end down. Starting halfway down the cob, use a sharp chef's knife to saw the kernels off the cob without cutting into the cob itself. Flip the cob over so the opposite end is down and shave off the remaining kernels. Repeat with the remaining ears of corn. Set the kernels aside and reserve the cobs. Run the dull (top) side of the chef's knife over the cobs over a plate to catch as much of the remaining juice and pulp from the cobs as possible.

2. Transfer the juice and pulp to a large soup pot or Dutch oven, and add the cobs (snap or cut in half so they fit in the pot), 6 cups [1.4 L] cold water, the peppercorns, bay leaves, and thyme sprigs and bring to a boil over high heat. Reduce the heat to medium-low and simmer, uncovered, for 20 minutes. Strain the broth through a fine-mesh sieve into a large bowl and discard the solids.

CONTINUED

73

3. Return the pot to medium heat, and melt the butter. Add the corn kernels, onion, 1 tsp salt, and cayenne and cook, stirring frequently, until the onion is translucent, about 10 minutes. Add the strained corn broth and simmer, uncovered, for 10 minutes.

4. Purée the soup in the pot with an immersion blender, or in batches in a blender with the lid slightly ajar to allow steam to escape. Strain the soup through a fine-mesh sieve and return it to the pot. Add the buttermilk, season with salt and pepper, and cook over low heat until just warmed through. Do not boil the soup or it may curdle. Divide the soup among individual bowls. Top each serving with crab, bacon, and a few of the spinach leaves.

GET AHEAD: The soup, without the garnishes, can be cooled and stored in airtight containers or zip-top plastic freezer bags in the refrigerator for up to 4 days, or in the freezer for up to 3 months. Defrost overnight in the refrigerator and reheat over low heat until hot. If the soup separates, blend it in the pot with an immersion blender or in a blender with the lid slightly ajar.

SERVES

4 TO 6

ACTIVE TIME

30

MINUTES

TOTAL TIME

60

MINUTES

This is perhaps the most involved recipe in the book since it requires making a lobster broth in addition to puréeing and straining the soup. That said, it's lots less fiddly than traditional French recipes that require cooking and shelling live whole lobsters. I use lobster tails instead, which lend the soup plenty of flavor without the work of shelling lobster. The reward for a bit of effort is a decadent soup that is bound to become a favorite in your soup repertoire.

The Gruyère pastry puffs on page 166 match the sophisticated flavors in this ritzy soup, but if you're not feeling fancy, crisp Pilot Biscuits (page 143) are also a good match.

Lobster Tail Bisque

PAIR WITH

Gruyère Cheese Choux Pastry Puffs (PAGE 166)
Pilot Biscuits (PAGE 143)

Four 6-oz [170-g] lobster tails
2 Tbsp unsalted butter
3 large shallots, thinly sliced
1 large carrot, peeled and
    finely chopped
2 tsp chopped fresh thyme
3 Tbsp tomato paste
1 medium garlic clove, minced
½ cup [120 ml] dry white wine
3 cups [720 ml] seafood broth
3 Tbsp all-purpose flour
1 cup [240 ml] heavy cream,
    warmed until hot to the touch
3 Tbsp Cognac or a similar brandy
1½ Tbsp chopped fresh tarragon
1 Tbsp freshly squeezed lime juice
Sea salt
Ground white pepper

1. Cleave the lobster tails in half lengthwise: using a sharp chef's knife, cut down the length of the underside of each lobster tail by plunging the tip of the knife about 1 in [2.5 cm] from the end of the tail and then pushing through the flesh and the shell, leaning on the knife to break through the shell. (Alternatively, use sharp kitchen shears to cut through the shell on both sides and then cut the tail in half.) Set aside.

2. Melt the butter in a large soup pot or Dutch oven over medium heat. Add the shallots, carrot, and thyme and sauté until the shallots are translucent, about 4 minutes. Add the tomato paste and garlic and cook, stirring constantly, until fragrant, about 45 seconds. Add the wine and simmer until the wine has reduced by half, about 1 minute.

3. Add the seafood broth and lobster tails to the pot, cover, and bring to a simmer. Reduce the heat to low and simmer gently until the lobster meat is opaque throughout, about 10 minutes. Remove the lobster tails from the pot, transfer to a cutting board, and let cool for a few minutes. Remove the meat from the shells by plunging a fork into the meat, twisting and pulling until it releases from its shell. Chop the tail meat into bite-size pieces, reserving a few of the most attractive pieces to garnish each bowl. Discard the shells.

4. In a small bowl, whisk together the flour with ¼ cup [60 ml] water until smooth. Add the flour mixture to the pot, bring to a simmer, and cook, uncovered, until the soup thickens a bit, about 2 minutes.

Return the lobster meat (except for the garnish pieces) to the pot. Purée the soup in the pot with an immersion blender, or in batches in a blender with the lid ajar until smooth.

5. Strain the soup through a mesh sieve into a large bowl, pressing on the solids with a rubber spatula to get out as much liquid as possible; discard the solids. Return the soup to the pot and add the cream, brandy, and 1 Tbsp of the tarragon. Cook over medium-low heat, stirring occasionally, until the soup is hot, about 4 minutes. Add the lime juice and season with salt and pepper.

6. Ladle the soup into bowls and garnish each serving with the reserved lobster meat and some of the remaining ½ Tbsp tarragon. Serve immediately.

GET AHEAD: You can make the bisque up to 1 day in advance. Return the lobster shells to the cooled soup to further infuse the soup with flavor, and refrigerate. To finish, remove the shells and reheat gently over low heat. The bisque also freezes well. Store in airtight containers or zip-top plastic freezer bags for up to 3 months. Reheat the soup in a covered saucepan over low heat (do not boil or the lobster meat will become tough). Add a squeeze of lime juice to the soup before serving to brighten the flavor.

SERVES

4 TO 6

ACTIVE TIME

15

MINUTES

TOTAL TIME

45

MINUTES

I originally devised this seafood-rich soup while surf-camping on the Oregon coast, where I'd cook local seafood over a campfire with shelf-stable V-8 tomato juice and bottled clam juice. I've since brought the recipe indoors and gussied it up with fresh fennel, thyme, and saffron, but one whiff of this cioppino and I can hear the waves crashing on my favorite lonesome Pacific beach.

For a more rustic (and thriftier) presentation, use crab legs and quartered body pieces instead of picked crab meat. Just remember to put out crab crackers and extra napkins!

Crab, Halibut, and Squid Cioppino

PAIR WITH

Quick Flatbread with Anchovy Butter (PAGE 135)

2 Tbsp extra-virgin olive oil
1 large yellow onion, chopped
1 medium fennel bulb, cored
  and chopped
4 medium garlic cloves, minced
1 Tbsp chopped fresh thyme
1 cup [240 ml] dry white wine
2 pinches of saffron
4 cups [960 ml] clam juice
  or seafood broth
2 cups [480 ml] V8 tomato juice
One 9-oz [255-g] baking potato,
  peeled and cut into half-moon
  slices ¼ in [6 mm] thick
Pinch of red chile flakes
2 bay leaves

1 lb [455 g] firm white-fleshed
  fish, such as halibut, cut into
  ½-in [12-mm] chunks
8 oz [230 g] lump crabmeat, picked
  over, or 1 cooked Dungeness crab,
  body quartered, legs broken into
  manageable pieces
8 oz [230 g] cleaned squid,
  bodies sliced into rounds
  ¼ in [6 mm] thick
1 Tbsp chopped fresh tarragon
Sea salt
Freshly ground black pepper
Lemon wedges, for serving

1. Heat the oil in a large soup pot or Dutch oven over medium-high heat. Add the onion and fennel and sauté, stirring frequently, until the onion is translucent, about 5 minutes. Add the garlic and thyme and cook until fragrant, about 45 seconds.

2. Add the wine to the pot, crumble the saffron into it, and cook until the wine has evaporated by half, about 3 minutes. Add the clam juice, tomato juice, potato, red chile flakes, and bay leaves. Bring to a boil. Reduce the heat to medium-low, cover, and simmer until the potato is just tender, about 15 minutes.

3. Add the fish and cook until just cooked through and opaque in the center, 6 minutes. Add the crabmeat, squid, and tarragon and cook gently until the squid is just cooked through, 2 to 3 minutes; do not boil or the squid will become rubbery. Remove the pot from the heat and season with salt and pepper.

4. Ladle the soup into bowls and serve with lemon wedges on the side.

GET AHEAD: The broth mixture (without seafood) can easily be doubled and stored in air-tight containers or zip-top plastic freezer bags in the freezer for up to 3 months. Defrost overnight in the refrigerator and reheat over medium heat until simmering before adding the seafood as directed.

Leftover soup with seafood can be stored in the refrigerator for up to 1 day. Reheat it very gently over low heat or the squid will become tough.

SERVES

4 TO 6

ACTIVE TIME

25 MINUTES

TOTAL TIME

45 MINUTES

This easy Brazilian fish stew, called moqueca (mo-KEH-kah), is from the coastal state of Bahia, where fish, coconuts, and peppers are plentiful. I use local Pacific rockfish, but any sustainable, firm white-fleshed fish, such as halibut or true cod, will do. If bay scallops or crab are in season, you can substitute them for the shrimp. In Brazil, the recipe varies from kitchen to kitchen, depending on what the catch of the day is.

This creamy-spicy soup teams up well with the other Brazilian recipe in this book, the cheesy tapioca rolls on page 165.

Brazilian Seafood and Coconut Soup

PAIR WITH

Brazilian Tapioca and Cheese Rolls (PAGE 165)

1 lb [455 g] firm white-fleshed fish, skin and bones removed
8 oz [230 g] medium shrimp, peeled and deveined
¼ cup [60 ml] freshly squeezed lime juice
Sea salt
1½ Tbsp coconut oil or safflower oil
1 medium onion, finely chopped
1 red bell pepper, seeded and chopped
1 yellow bell pepper, seeded and chopped
1 serrano chile, finely chopped
2 medium garlic cloves, minced
2 Tbsp minced fresh ginger
2 medium plum tomatoes, finely chopped
1 tsp sweet paprika
One 13½-oz [400-ml] can coconut milk
1 cup [240 ml] fish broth or bottled clam juice
1 bay leaf
Freshly ground black pepper
¼ cup [7 g] chopped fresh cilantro

1. Place the fish and shrimp in a large zip-top plastic bag, add the lime juice and 1 tsp salt, and toss to coat the seafood. Marinate at room temperature for 30 minutes.

2. Meanwhile, heat the coconut oil in a large sauté pan or in a Dutch oven over medium heat. Add the onion, bell peppers, and chile and sauté until the vegetables are tender, about 8 minutes. Add the garlic and ginger and sauté until fragrant, about 45 seconds. Add the tomatoes and paprika and cook for 1 minute. Add the coconut milk, fish broth, and bay leaf. Cover, reduce the heat to medium-low, and simmer gently until the flavors have melded, about 10 minutes.

3. Add the fish, shrimp, and their marinade to the pot and stir gently, making sure that the seafood is almost completely covered with the broth mixture. Simmer, uncovered, stirring gently only once, until the seafood is just cooked; the fish chunks will flake easily with a fork and the shrimp will be curled and pink, about 8 minutes. Discard the bay leaf and season the soup with salt and pepper.

4. Serve the soup in bowls, sprinkled with the cilantro.

GET AHEAD: The broth (without the seafood) can be made in advance and stored in air-tight containers in the refrigerator for up to 4 days, or in zip-top bags in the freezer up to 3 months. Defrost the broth overnight in the refrigerator. Marinate the seafood while you're reheating the soup, and cook as directed above.

SERVES

4

ACTIVE TIME

15

MINUTES

TOTAL TIME

30

MINUTES

If you love linguini and clams in red sauce, then you'll love this Sicilian soup. The pasta ribbons are replaced by small, BB-size toasted pasta called fregola, which simmers in a saucy broth of garlic, anchovies, seafood broth, and good-quality jarred marinara sauce. It's lightning-quick and ticks all the boxes when I'm craving Mediterranean shellfish.

I love to soak up the briny broth with a roll wrapped in salty prosciutto (see page 163) or a wedge of garlicky focaccia (see page 142), but on really lazy nights, a slice of buttered toast sprinkled with garlic powder will do the trick.

Spicy Sicilian Clam Soup with Fregola

PAIR WITH

Olive and Prosciutto Rolls (PAGE 163)
Roasted Garlic Focaccia (PAGE 142)

3 lb [1.4 kg] Manila or littleneck clams
2 Tbsp extra-virgin olive oil
1 medium yellow onion, finely chopped
3 large garlic cloves, thinly sliced
3 oil-packed anchovies
½ cup [120 ml] dry white wine
4 cups [960 ml] seafood broth,
    bottled clam juice, or
    chicken broth (see page 17)
1½ cups [360 ml] marinara sauce
    from a jar
¾ cup [135 g] fregola pasta or
    Israeli couscous
1 Tbsp chopped fresh oregano,
    or 1¼ tsp dried oregano
2 pinches red chile flakes
Sea salt
Freshly ground black pepper
3 Tbsp finely chopped fresh
    Italian parsley
1 lemon, cut into 6 wedges

1. Place the clams in a large bowl of cold water and swish gently to dislodge any grit. Drain and repeat with two more changes of water. Discard any clams with cracked shells, or shells that do not close when tapped. Drain the clams and place them in the refrigerator, covered with a damp paper towel, until ready to cook.

2. Heat the oil in a large soup pot or Dutch oven over medium-high heat. Add the onion and sauté until it begins to brown, about 4 minutes. Add the garlic and anchovies and cook, stirring constantly until fragrant, about 30 seconds.

3. Add the wine to the pot and cook until half of it has evaporated, about 1 minute. Add the seafood broth, marinara sauce, fregola, oregano, and red chile flakes. Cover and bring to a simmer. Reduce the heat to medium-low and simmer, stirring occasionally, until the fregola is just tender, about 8 minutes.

CONTINUED

4. Gently fold the clams into the broth mixture, cover, and simmer until the clams open, 5 to 8 minutes. Check frequently and don't overcook the clams; they will become rubbery quite quickly. Discard any clams that don't open. Season with salt and pepper.

5. Ladle the soup into bowls, sprinkle with the parsley, and serve with the lemon wedges.

GET AHEAD: You can make the broth (without the clams) and store in airtight containers or zip-top plastic freezer bags in the refrigerator for up to 4 days, or in the freezer for up to 3 months. Reheat the broth gently. Add a bit of water or shellfish broth if necessary to adjust the consistency. Add the clams once the broth begins to simmer and proceed as directed.

This clam chowder is unapologetically rich. Adapted from a recipe by Chef Mike Parameter of Old Lompoc Brewery, his chunky, cream-based soup has taken the prize at the brewery's annual Chowder Challenge six times for good reason. There's not a lot of bells and whistles here, just straightforward clam flavor thanks to clam juice, good-quality canned clams, and a judicious amount of butter and cream.

I like to pair this simple soup with puffy, crispy Pilot Biscuits (page 143), the granddaddy of oyster crackers.

SERVES

4 TO 6

ACTIVE TIME

15 MINUTES

TOTAL TIME

45 MINUTES

Creamy New England–Style Clam Chowder

PAIR WITH

Pilot Biscuits (PAGE 143)

1 strip thick-cut pepper bacon, diced
1 medium yellow onion, finely chopped
3 celery stalks, thinly sliced
½ cup [120 ml] dry white wine
5 Tbsp [70 g] unsalted butter
½ cup plus 2 Tbsp [90 g]
    all-purpose flour
3 cups [720 ml] clam juice or seafood
    broth
3 cups [720 ml] heavy cream
Two 10-oz [280-g] cans
    baby clams with juice
One 10-oz [280-g] baking potato,
    peeled and cut into
    ½-in [12-mm] dice
2 tsp chopped fresh thyme
2 pinches of cayenne pepper
Celery salt or Old Bay seasoning
Freshly ground black pepper

1. Cook the bacon in a large soup pot or Dutch oven over medium-low heat, stirring frequently, until the fat has rendered and the bacon is crisp, about 3 minutes. Reduce the heat if the bacon begins to scorch. Add the onion and celery and increase the heat to medium. Sauté until the onion is translucent, about 4 minutes. Add the wine and cook until the liquid has nearly evaporated, about 1 minute.

2. Add the butter to the vegetables and, when it has melted, add the flour and cook, stirring constantly, for 1 minute. Gradually whisk in the clam juice and bring to a simmer. Add the cream, the clams and their juice, the potato, and the thyme. Cover and bring the soup to a gentle simmer, stirring frequently so the soup does not stick to the bottom of the pot. Reduce the heat to low and simmer gently until the soup has thickened and the potato is tender, about 10 minutes. Season with the cayenne, celery salt, and pepper.

3. Ladle the soup into bowls and serve immediately.

GET AHEAD: Cool the chowder completely and store in airtight containers or zip-top plastic freezer bags in the refrigerator for up to 3 days. You can freeze this soup for up to 3 months, but like all chowders, the texture will change a bit. Defrost the soup in the refrigerator overnight. If the sight of a slightly separated soup bothers you, strain the soup, reserving the solids, and whiz the broth in a blender. Combine the broth and the reserved solids in a pot and reheat very gently over low heat.

SERVES

4 TO 6

ACTIVE TIME

15

MINUTES

TOTAL TIME

40

MINUTES

This is a much lighter chowder than the New England clam chowder on page 85. It's more typical of Pacific Northwest chowders in that it includes wild smoked salmon and raw salmon chunks and a light broth of seafood broth, craft beer, and milk instead of cream. I use 2 percent milk, but whatever you have on hand will work. I love the way the fresh flavors of celery and celery root cut through the richness of the salmon.

This soup is best when served with a fistful of yeasty, crunchy Pilot Biscuits (page 143) crumbled on top, but the presence of sage points to the bannock bread on page 153 as well.

Smoked Salmon and Celery Root Chowder

PAIR WITH

Pilot Biscuits (PAGE 143)
Bannock Bread with Browned Butter and Sage (PAGE 153)

3 cups [720 ml] milk
1 bay leaf
2 Tbsp extra-virgin olive oil
1 large yellow onion, finely chopped
2 celery stalks, thinly sliced
1 medium garlic clove, minced
1 Tbsp chopped fresh sage, or 1 tsp
     dried sage leaves
5 Tbsp [50 g] all-purpose flour
3 cups [720 ml] seafood broth or
     bottled clam juice
1 cup [240 ml] craft lager beer
1 large celery root, peeled and cut
     into ¼-in [6-mm] pieces
8 oz [225 g] red potato (1 large),
     unpeeled, cut into
     ¼-in [6-mm] pieces
6 oz [170 g] boneless, skinless wild
     salmon, cut into bite-size chunks
4 oz [115 g] cold smoked salmon,
     chopped
Pinch of cayenne pepper
Sea salt
Freshly ground black pepper
2 Tbsp chopped fresh Italian parsley

1. Combine the milk and bay leaf in a large measuring cup or a microwave-safe bowl and microwave on high heat until hot, about 2 minutes. (Alternatively, heat the milk and bay leaf in a small saucepan over low heat until hot, about 10 minutes.) Set aside and allow the bay leaf to steep in the milk while starting the soup.

2. Heat the olive oil in a large soup pot or Dutch oven over medium heat. Add the onion and celery and cook, stirring occasionally, until the onion is translucent, about 8 minutes. Add the garlic and sage and cook, stirring constantly, until fragrant, about 45 seconds. Add the flour and stir constantly for 1 minute more.

3. Discard the bay leaf in the milk. Whisk the milk and seafood broth into the flour and onion mixture and bring to a simmer, stirring constantly. Add the beer, celery root, and potato, and return to a gentle simmer. Reduce the heat to low and simmer, stirring frequently, until the celery root and potato are tender and the soup has thickened, 10 minutes. Watch the heat closely and reduce it

if necessary to prevent the soup from scorching on the bottom of the pot.

4. Add the raw and smoked salmon and cook until the raw salmon is opaque in the center of the largest chunk, about 3 minutes. Add the cayenne and season with salt and pepper.

5. Ladle the chowder into soup bowls and sprinkle with the parsley. Serve immediately.

GET AHEAD: The soup, without the fish, can be stored in airtight containers or zip-top plastic freezer bags in the refrigerator for up to 3 days, or in the freezer for up to 3 months. (See the Get Ahead note on page 85 for tips on regaining the correct texture.) To reheat, defrost the frozen soup overnight in the refrigerator, bring to a very gentle simmer, and then add the salmon.

Imagine rich, briny mussels clattering around in a smoky, aromatic broth of hard cider, shallots, bacon, and cream that's ready in 20 minutes. What's not to love? This recipe is so simple that it pays to be picky when shopping for the ingredients. Don't buy mussels if they look dry or if lots of them are gasping with open shells; they should look moist, the shells should have no cracks, and they should be mostly closed. Also, buy the best bacon you can and choose a cider you would be happy to drink on its own.

Mussel Stew with Bacon, Cider, and Cream

PAIR WITH

Beer and Cheddar Bread (PAGE 157)

2½ lb [1.2 kg] **mussels**
1 Tbsp **extra-virgin olive oil**
3 large **shallots, peeled and thinly sliced**
2 strips **thick-cut bacon, coarsely chopped**
1 large **garlic clove, thinly sliced**
1 Tbsp **chopped fresh thyme**
2 cups [480 ml] **dry hard apple cider**
2 cups [480 ml] **heavy cream**
Sea salt
Freshly ground black pepper

1. Place the mussels in a large bowl of cold water, and swish them gently to expel sand and grit. Drain and repeat. Immediately before cooking, pull off and discard the tough, fibrous "beards" protruding from the sides of their shells. Discard any mussels with cracked shells or ones that don't close up when lightly squeezed.

Cover the mussels with a wet paper towel and set them aside in the refrigerator while preparing the broth.

2. Heat the oil in a large soup pot or Dutch oven over medium heat. Add the shallots and bacon and sauté until the shallots are translucent and the bacon is beginning to brown, 5 to 8 minutes. Add the garlic and thyme and cook, stirring constantly, until fragrant, about 45 seconds.

3. Add the cider and cream to the pot and bring to a simmer over medium-high heat. Add the mussels, stir gently to combine, cover, and simmer until the mussels have opened, 3 to 5 minutes. Remove the pot from the heat, discard any unopened mussels, and season the soup with salt and pepper.

4. Ladle the stew into bowls and provide an empty bowl for diners to discard the shells.

GET AHEAD: The stew is best served immediately. Should you have any leftovers, remove the mussels from their shells and return them to the stew, discarding the shells. Store the cooled soup in airtight containers in the refrigerator for up to 1 day. Reheat gently or the mussels will become rubbery.

Meat and Poultry Soups

A specialty of the Emilia-Romagna region of Italy, this soup is the very definition of simplicity—fresh tortellini bobbing in a rich meat broth infused with a chunk of Parmigiano-Reggiano cheese rind. It's elegant enough for a special occasion, but it's easy enough to throw together on a hectic weeknight when you need a bowl of comfort. I doctor up the traditional pasta-broth equation a bit by adding shredded chicken breast and a handful of whatever vegetables are in season. In winter that means Lacinato kale ribbons and carrot coins, and in autumn I'll use sliced wild mushrooms. Come spring, I'll throw in fresh shelled peas or asparagus tips, and in summer, I'll float a few halved heirloom cherry tomatoes and basil leaves in the broth.

SERVES

4 TO 6

ACTIVE TIME

10

MINUTES

TOTAL TIME

40

MINUTES

Tortellini Chicken Soup with Seasonal Vegetables

PAIR WITH

Roasted Garlic Focaccia (PAGE 142)

8 cups [2 L] chicken broth
   (see page 17)
8 oz [230 g] boneless, skinless
   chicken breasts
One 3-in [7.5-cm] chunk Parmigiano-
   Reggiano cheese rind
1 bay leaf
One 9-oz [255-g] package fresh
   tortellini
Generous handful of seasonal
   vegetables (see headnote)
Sea salt
Freshly ground black pepper

1. In a large soup pot or Dutch oven, combine the chicken broth, chicken breasts, cheese rind, and bay leaf. Bring to a very gentle simmer over medium-low heat; do not boil or the chicken will become dry and cottony. Reduce the heat to low and cook, uncovered, until an instant-read thermometer reaches 165°F [74°C] when inserted into the thickest part of the chicken breast, or the meat is no longer pink in the thickest part, about 20 minutes. Transfer the chicken to a cutting board, shred or chop the meat, and set aside.

CONTINUED

2. Increase the heat to medium-high and add the tortellini and vegetables. Simmer gently, uncovered, until the pasta is tender and the vegetables are done to your liking, about 8 minutes. Discard the cheese rind and bay leaf. Return the chicken to the pot, cook for 1 minute to reheat the chicken, and season with salt and pepper.

3. Serve immediately; the soup looks best in shallow white bowls, so diners can fully appreciate the colorful vegetables and clear broth.

GET AHEAD: You can store the cooled broth (with the chopped chicken, cheese rind, and bay leaf) in airtight containers or zip-top plastic freezer bags in the refrigerator for up to 4 days, or in the freezer for up to 3 months. To finish, reheat the soup and add the tortellini and vegetables as directed.

SERVES

4 TO **6**

ACTIVE TIME

15

MINUTES

TOTAL TIME

35

MINUTES

I learned to make this velvety chicken soup spiked with lemon, called avgolemono *in Greek, while I was an exchange student in the lovely port town of Kavala, in northern Greece. The soup is thickened with eggs and it can be tricky to make without the soup curdling, but my Greek host-mother taught me to add a bit of cornstarch to the eggs before tempering them with some of the soup to stabilize the mixture. The result is a thick, rich soup that's nearly foolproof. You can substitute white long-grain rice for the orzo pasta for gluten-free soup. Add the rice to the pot along with the broth in step 2.*

The Zucchini, Feta, and Dill Muffins (page 168) have a springlike, lemony flavor similar to the soup, and they serve as an excellent sponge for cleaning up the last bites at the bottom of the bowl.

Egg and Lemon Soup with Toasted Orzo and Kale

PAIR WITH

Zucchini, Feta, and Dill Muffins (PAGE 168)

2 Tbsp unsalted butter
¾ cup [115 g] orzo pasta
1 large leek, white and light green
    parts only, halved lengthwise, well
    rinsed, and thinly sliced
1 medium garlic clove, minced
7 cups [1.7 L] chicken broth
    (see page 17)
2 cups [270g] shredded rotisserie
    chicken meat
One 3-in [7.5-cm] chunk Parmigiano-
    Reggiano cheese rind
3 large eggs
1½ tsp finely grated lemon zest,
    plus 3 Tbsp freshly squeezed
    lemon juice
2 Tbsp chopped fresh dill
1 Tbsp cornstarch
1½ cups [115 g] thinly sliced Lacinato
    kale (optional; remove center rib
    before slicing)
Sea salt
Freshly ground black pepper

1. Melt the butter in a large soup pot or Dutch oven over medium heat. Add the orzo and cook, stirring frequently, until the pasta begins to turn golden brown in places, about 1 minute. Add the leek and cook, stirring frequently, until it is tender and the pasta is golden brown all over, about 3 minutes. Add the garlic and cook until fragrant, about 45 seconds.

2. Add the chicken broth, chicken meat, and cheese rind to the pot, cover, and bring to a simmer. Reduce the heat to low and simmer gently, stirring frequently to make sure the pasta doesn't catch on the bottom of the pot, until the pasta is just tender, about 5 minutes. Uncover the pot.

3. In a medium bowl, whisk the eggs, lemon zest, lemon juice, dill, and cornstarch. Whisk 1 cup [240 ml] of the hot soup into the egg mixture, and pour the mixture back into the soup. Add the kale (if using) and cook, stirring constantly in one direction until the soup thickens and the kale is tender, about 4 minutes. Season with salt and pepper.

4. Ladle the soup into bowls and serve immediately.

GET AHEAD: You can store the soup in airtight containers in the refrigerator for up to 3 days, or in zip-top plastic freezer bags in the freezer for up to 3 months, though the texture will become thicker and creamier (not necessarily a bad thing). Defrost overnight in the refrigerator and reheat the soup over low heat. Adjust the consistency with additional broth and brighten with a bit of lemon juice.

This comfort-food classic usually involves simmering a whole chicken for hours, skimming the broth, pulling the meat off the bones . . . in short, hours of work. To expedite the recipe and still have homemade flavor, I roast chicken thighs in a hot oven while the vegetable stew simmers, and then chop the meat and add it to the soup. The result is rich chicken soup like Grandma used to make—maybe even better. For an even quicker meal, use rotisserie chicken instead of roasting chicken thighs.

The soup can be served by itself, but I find the best bread pairing for this soup is one that's cooked right in the broth: light, herb-flecked dumplings (see page 150). The one-bowl dumpling recipe is a cinch to make and yields fluffy dumplings with a sprightly little kick of lemon zest and herbs; it's light but sticks to your ribs at the same time. If you're really in a hurry, substitute thick Pennsylvania Dutch-style kluski egg noodles instead. Add the dry noodles to the soup and simmer, stirring frequently, until tender, about 10 minutes.

Soulful Chicken Soup

PAIR WITH

Featherlight Herb Dumplings (PAGE 150)

6 bone-in chicken thighs, with skin
    (about 2¼ lb [1 kg])
Sea salt
Freshly ground black pepper
1 Tbsp extra-virgin olive oil
1 large leek, white and light green
    parts only, halved lengthwise, well
    rinsed, and thinly sliced
2 large carrots, peeled and thinly
    sliced into coins
2 celery stalks, thinly sliced
1 parsnip, peeled and chopped
1 Tbsp chopped fresh sage,
    or 1½ tsp dried sage leaves
1 medium garlic clove, minced
½ cup [120 ml] dry sherry or dry
    white wine
7 cups [1.7 L] chicken broth
    (see page 17)
2 Tbsp nutritional yeast
1 bay leaf

1 recipe Featherlight Herb Dumplings
    batter (page 150), or 6 oz [170 g]
    dried Pennsylvania Dutch kluski egg
    noodles (optional, see headnote)
2 Tbsp chopped fresh Italian parsley

1. Preheat the oven to 425°F [220°C]. Line a rimmed baking sheet with parchment paper.

2. Season the chicken thighs all over with salt and pepper and arrange in an even layer on the prepared baking sheet. Roast until an instant-read thermometer inserted into the center of a thigh registers 165°F [74°C], 20 to 30 minutes.

3. While the chicken roasts, heat the olive oil in a large soup pot or Dutch oven over medium heat. Add the leek, carrots, celery, and parsnip and cook, stirring frequently, until the vegetables begin to brown, about 8 minutes. Add the sage and garlic and cook, stirring constantly, until fragrant, about 45 seconds.

4. Add the sherry to the pot and cook, scraping up the browned bits on the bottom of the pan, until the liquid has evaporated, about 1 minute. Add the chicken broth, nutritional yeast, and bay leaf. Cover and bring to a simmer over medium heat. Reduce the heat to low and continue to simmer while the chicken is roasting.

5. When the chicken is cooked, transfer the pieces to a cutting board. Remove the skin and discard. Using a fork and knife, cut the meat away from the bones and chop it into bite-size pieces. Add the meat to the soup and bring to a simmer, uncovered. As the soup begins to bubble, excess fat will accumulate in clear or frothy pools on top the soup; use a soup spoon to skim off this fat as best you can. Season with salt and pepper.

6. Add the dumpling batter (if using) to the soup by heaping soupspoons, cover, and simmer gently until a skewer comes out clean when inserted into the center of a dumpling, about 10 to 12 minutes. (Do not boil or simmer the soup too vigorously or the dumplings will break up and disintegrate.) If using the kluski noodles, add them to the pot now and simmer until tender, 10 minutes.

7. Sprinkle the soup with the parsley, ladle into bowls, and serve immediately.

GET AHEAD: The soup (without dumplings or noodles) freezes well and the recipe doubles easily. To make a double batch of soup and save half for later, proceed with the recipe, doubling all the ingredients except the dumplings or noodles (if using). Set half of the soup aside before adding the dumplings or noodles. Cool the reserved soup completely and store in airtight containers or zip-top plastic freezer bags for up to 4 days in the refrigerator or up to 3 months in the freezer. Reheat the soup gently and add the dumpling batter or noodles once the soup is simmering.

Called tom kha gai *in Thai, this soup is named for the camphor-scented galangal root (kha). You can find galangal (it looks like ginger on steroids) and fresh lime leaves at Asian markets. Both freeze well, so stock up and you'll be set for months! There is no substitute for galangal, but it is present in most Thai curry pastes, so if you can't find galangal, include an extra 1 tsp or so of curry paste. This soup is brothy and light; if you prefer richer soup, substitute a can of thick coconut cream for one of the cans of coconut milk in the recipe.*

Thai Coconut Chicken Soup

PAIR WITH

Flaky Green Onion Pancakes (PAGE 139)
Korean Egg Breads (PAGE 162)

Two 15-oz [445-ml] cans coconut milk
2½ cups [600 ml] chicken broth
   (see page 17)
4 oz [115 g] oyster mushrooms or
   shiitake mushrooms (stems
   discarded if using shiitake), sliced
3 medium shallots, thinly sliced
¼ cup [35 g] thinly sliced
   fresh galangal root
2 tsp Thai red curry paste
2 tsp brown sugar
10 fresh lime leaves
1¼ lb [570 g] boneless, skinless
   chicken breasts, thinly sliced
   against the grain
3 Tbsp fish sauce
2 Tbsp freshly squeezed lime juice
¼ cup [7 g] chopped fresh cilantro

1. In a large soup pot or Dutch oven combine the coconut milk, chicken broth, mushrooms, shallots, galangal root, curry paste, brown sugar, and lime leaves. Bring the mixture to a boil over high heat. Reduce the heat to medium-low and simmer, uncovered, for 20 minutes to infuse the broth with the aromatics.

2. Add the chicken to the pot and cook over very low heat until the chicken is just cooked through, 5 to 10 minutes. Do not simmer the broth, or the chicken will become cottony and dry. Add the fish sauce and lime juice to the pot.

3. Ladle the soup into bowls and sprinkle with the cilantro. Instruct diners to pick out the galangal slices and lime leaves; they are too tough to eat.

GET AHEAD: Store the cooled soup in airtight containers or zip-top plastic freezer bags for up to 4 days in the refrigerator or up to 3 months in the freezer. Defrost overnight before reheating over low heat. Add the cilantro immediately before serving.

SERVES

4 TO 6

ACTIVE TIME

10
MINUTES

TOTAL TIME

35
MINUTES

This zesty chicken noodle soup, called sopa de fideos *in Mexico, is definitely not your mom's chicken noodle soup—unless your mom happens to be Mexican, in which case this soup will be very comforting and familiar. Chicken breasts are poached in a smoky, limey broth swimming with nutty, toasted vermicelli noodle nests and decorated with fresh cilantro and avocado—just the thing to brighten a dreary winter day. Look for* fideos *pasta with Mexican ingredients in grocery stores, or substitute broken angel hair pasta in a pinch.*

Mexican Chicken Noodle Soup

PAIR WITH

Homemade Corn Tortillas (PAGE 140)

2 Tbsp extra-virgin olive oil
1 small yellow onion, finely chopped
2 Tbsp tomato paste
2 medium garlic cloves, thinly sliced
8 cups [2 L] chicken broth
    (see page 17)
1½ lb [680 g] boneless, skinless
    chicken breast halves, fat trimmed
1 Tbsp chopped canned
    chipotle chiles in adobo
2 tsp chopped fresh oregano,
    or 1 tsp dried Mexican oregano
Pinch of saffron
6 oz [170 g] fideos noodle nests
    or broken angel hair pasta
2 Tbsp freshly squeezed lime juice,
    plus 1 lime, cut into 6 wedges
Sea salt
Freshly ground black pepper
¼ cup [7 g] chopped fresh cilantro
1 ripe avocado, pitted, peeled,
    and diced

1. Heat 1 Tbsp of the olive oil in a large soup pot or Dutch oven over medium heat. Add the onion and sauté until translucent, about 3 minutes. Add the tomato paste and garlic and continue to cook until the garlic is aromatic and the tomato paste begins to brown a little, about 30 seconds. Add the chicken broth, chicken breasts, chipotles, oregano, and saffron. Cover and bring to a simmer. Reduce the heat to very low and simmer gently until the chicken is cooked through or an instant-read thermometer inserted into the thickest part of the chicken reads 165°F [74°C], about 10 minutes. Do not boil or the chicken will become dry and cottony.

2. While the soup simmers, toast the noodles. In a large skillet, heat the remaining 1 Tbsp olive oil over medium heat. When the oil shimmers, add the noodles and cook, stirring constantly, until deep golden brown, about 4 minutes. Scrape the noodles into a bowl and set aside.

3. When the chicken is cooked, transfer it to a cutting board and chop it into bite-size pieces. Return the chicken to the soup, add the toasted noodles, and continue to simmer, uncovered, until the noodles are just tender, about 5 minutes.

4. Add the lime juice and season with salt and pepper.

5. Serve the soup in bowls, garnished with the cilantro and avocado, with the lime wedges on the side.

GET AHEAD: The soup can be made in advance, but omit the noodles and garnishes. Cool completely in the refrigerator before storing in airtight containers or zip-top plastic freezer bags in the refrigerator for up to 3 days, or in the freezer for up to 3 months. To finish, reheat the soup, toast the noodles, and continue with the recipe as directed.

SERVES

4 TO 6

ACTIVE TIME

10

MINUTES

TOTAL TIME

40

MINUTES

This quick, restorative chicken soup is packed with anti-inflammatory ingredients like garlic, ginger, cumin, and turmeric, so it's a go-to when I've got the sniffles. I'm not wild about supermarket rotisserie chicken on its own, but it's a great shortcut here as a meaty garnish for the flavorful soup. (Don't forget to add the juices in the bottom of the chicken container—they add a good flavor boost to the broth.) Or, if you happen to have leftover turkey kicking around in the refrigerator, this is an excellent home for it. Make sure your curry powder is fresh; stale curry powder yields a flat-tasting soup.

Soft net breads (see page 147), often served with chicken curry in Malaysia, are a fitting side dish for this sweet-spicy soup.

Spicy Sweet Chicken Curry Soup

PAIR WITH

Malaysian Net Breads (PAGE 147)

2 Tbsp safflower or coconut oil
2 large carrots, peeled and chopped
1 large yellow onion, chopped
1 medium Fuji apple, peeled, cored, and chopped
2 Tbsp minced fresh ginger
3 medium garlic cloves, minced
1 Tbsp curry powder
4 cups [960 ml] chicken broth (see page 17)
One 12-oz [340-g] baking potato, peeled and chopped
2 lemongrass stalks, cut in half crosswise
2½ cups [340 g] skinless shredded rotisserie chicken, plus juices from bottom of container, or leftover turkey
2 Tbsp freshly squeezed lime juice
1 Tbsp plus 2 tsp soy sauce
1 tsp firmly packed brown sugar
Sea salt
Freshly ground black pepper

¼ cup plus 2 Tbsp [10 g] chopped fresh cilantro
¼ cup plus 2 Tbsp [25 g] fried shallots (see Flavor Toolbox, page 14)

1. Heat the oil in a large soup pot or Dutch oven over medium-high heat. Add the carrots, onion, and all but 2 Tbsp of the apple. Cover and cook, stirring occasionally, until the onion is translucent, about 5 minutes. Add the ginger, garlic, and curry powder and cook, uncovered, stirring constantly, for 30 seconds.

2. Add the chicken broth, 2 cups [480 ml] water, and the potato to the pot and bring to a simmer. Meanwhile, using a meat mallet or rolling pin, smack the lemongrass stalks once or twice to release the aromatic oils and add them to the pot. Cover the pot and reduce the heat to low. Simmer gently, stirring occasionally, until the potato is fall-apart tender, about 20 minutes.

3. Discard the lemongrass. Blend the soup in the pot with an immersion blender, or in batches in a blender with the lid slightly ajar to let steam escape, until the soup is smooth. Return the soup to the pot and set over medium-low heat.

4. Add the shredded chicken, lime juice, soy sauce, and brown sugar and cook until the chicken is heated through, about 2 minutes. Season with salt and pepper.

5. Divide the soup among bowls and garnish with the reserved apple, the cilantro, and fried shallots. Serve immediately.

GET AHEAD: An average-size supermarket rotisserie chicken will yield about 4 cups [550 g] of meat; you will need a little more than half of a bird for this recipe. The cooled soup (without the fried shallots, cilantro, or raw apple garnishes) can be kept in airtight containers or zip-top plastic freezer bags in the refrigerator for up to 4 days, or in the freezer for up to 3 months. Reheat the soup gently and then top with the garnishes.

SERVES

4 TO **6**

ACTIVE TIME

15

MINUTES

TOTAL TIME

35

MINUTES

This is a simple Italian recipe that is elegant enough to trot out for company, but takes less than 35 minutes to put together. As with most Italian dishes, the ingredients are simple, so you should use the very best to make the soup a success. If you have homemade chicken broth, this is the place to use it, though store-bought broth will work, too. As for the greens, I use a boxed blend of sturdy salad greens (arugula, tatsoi, baby kale, and baby Swiss chard leaves). If you can't find such a blend, chop up some Lacinato kale or escarole, or use a bag of baby spinach.

Italian Meatball and Greens Soup

PAIR WITH

Olive and Prosciutto Rolls (PAGE 163)
Roasted Garlic Focaccia (PAGE 142)

7 cups [1.7 L] chicken broth
   (see page 17)
One 2-in [5-cm] chunk Parmigiano-
   Reggiano cheese rind
1 bay leaf
1 large egg, beaten
3 Tbsp milk
2 Tbsp finely chopped fresh
   Italian parsley
4 medium garlic cloves, minced
2 tsp dried oregano
1½ tsp finely grated lemon zest,
   plus 2 Tbsp freshly squeezed
   lemon juice
Sea salt
Freshly ground black pepper
⅓ cup [30 g] panko bread crumbs
1 lb [455 g] ground dark-meat turkey
   or sustainably raised ground veal
3 cups [60 g] baby kale, Swiss chard,
   arugula, and/or baby tatsoi
   greens, loosely packed, chopped

1. Preheat the oven to 425°F [220°C]. Line a rimmed baking sheet with parchment paper or aluminum foil.

2. In a large soup pot or Dutch oven over medium-high heat, bring the chicken broth, cheese rind, and bay leaf to a simmer. Reduce the heat to low, cover, and simmer while you bake the meatballs.

3. In a medium bowl, whisk together the egg, milk, parsley, garlic, oregano, lemon zest, ¾ tsp salt, and ½ tsp pepper. Add the bread crumbs and stir until they are moistened. Add the ground meat and stir thoroughly to combine (I prefer to do this with clean or gloved hands to make sure everything is well blended). Form the mixture into thirty meatballs (about 1¼ Tbsp each) and arrange them on the prepared baking sheet. Bake until the meatballs are nearly cooked through but still a little pink in the middle, about 12 minutes.

4. Transfer the meatballs to the soup, leaving any extra fat behind on the baking sheet. Add the greens to the soup, cover, and cook until they are tender, about 10 minutes. Add the lemon juice and season with salt and pepper.

5. Discard the cheese rind and bay leaf, ladle the soup into bowls, and serve immediately.

GET AHEAD: The meatball recipe doubles easily, and the meatballs freeze well. Bake a double batch on two baking sheets. Freeze half of the par-baked meatballs until firm. Transfer the frozen meatballs to a zip-top plastic freezer bag and freeze for up to 3 months. To use, add the frozen meatballs to the soup as directed, adding 10 minutes to the simmering time. Cut a meatball in half to make sure it is heated through, or test with an instant-read thermometer to make sure they have reached 160°F [71°C]. The meatballs are also delicious simmered in marinara sauce and served with pasta.

SERVES

4 TO 6

ACTIVE TIME

15

MINUTES

TOTAL TIME

40

MINUTES

I wrote this recipe for my "Simply Affordable" column in the Oregonian news-paper as a way to use up post-Thanksgiving turkey, but I ended up loving the creamy, whole-grain soup so much, it's in regular rotation in our house now. If you don't have leftover turkey meat, roasted turkey breast or smoked turkey from the deli department will work. Ask them to cut you a thick slab, so you can cut it into bite-size cubes at home. The soup can be made vegetarian by omit-ting the meat and using vegetable broth. Just throw a few diced red potatoes into the soup with the wild rice, and you've got a hearty meat-free chowder. I like to dip wedges of crispy Bannock Bread with Browned Butter and Sage (page 153) into this soup; sage and wild rice are always good partners.

Creamy Wild Rice and Turkey Soup

PAIR WITH

Bannock Bread with Browned Butter and Sage (PAGE 153)

2 Tbsp unsalted butter
1 medium onion, finely chopped
2 celery stalks, thinly sliced
2 medium carrots, peeled and
  finely chopped
1½ cups [130 g] sliced cremini
  mushrooms
1 Tbsp chopped fresh savory,
  or ½ tsp dried savory
½ cup [120 ml] dry sherry or
  dry white wine
5 cups [1.2 L] chicken broth
  (see page 17)
3½ cups (1 lb/455 g) chopped
  roasted turkey breast
1½ cups [240 g] cooked wild rice,
  homemade (see Get Ahead) or
  store-bought (available in the
  freezer section of some
  grocery stores)
1 bay leaf
½ cup [70 g] all-purpose flour
1 cup [240 ml] heavy cream
1 Tbsp freshly squeezed lemon juice
Sea salt
Freshly ground black pepper

1. Melt the butter in a large soup pot or Dutch oven over medium-high heat. Add the onion, celery, carrots, mush-rooms, and savory and sauté until the onion is translucent, about 8 minutes.

2. Add the sherry to the pot and cook, scrap-ing up browned bits on the bottom of the pan, until the sherry has mostly evapo-rated, about 1 minute. Add 4 cups [960 ml] of the chicken broth, the turkey, wild rice, and bay leaf and bring to a simmer.

3. Place the flour in a medium bowl, and gradually whisk in the remaining 1 cup [240 ml] broth. Continue whisking until the mixture is smooth.

4. Add the flour mixture to the soup and bring to a simmer, stirring frequently. Reduce the heat to low, cover, and cook, stirring frequently, until the soup has thickened and the vegetables are tender, about 10 minutes. Add the cream and lemon juice and season with salt and pepper.

5. Ladle the soup into bowls and serve immediately.

CONTINUED

GET AHEAD: Wild rice is easy to make and freezes well. Follow the package cooking instructions and store the cooked and cooled rice in an airtight container in the refrigerator for up to 4 days or in zip-top freezer bags in the freezer for up to 3 months.

Store the soup in airtight containers in the refrigerator for up to 4 days or in zip-top plastic freezer bags in the freezer for up to 3 months. Defrost in the refrigerator overnight and reheat gently, covered, over low heat until hot.

This soup is more about the barley and the vegetables than about the beef, but the flavor is rich and meaty, thanks to red wine, beef broth, and a little strip steak seasoned with red miso paste. I use pearled barley here, but you can also use chewier whole-grain hulled barley; just add about 30 minutes to the cooking time.

SERVES
4 TO 6

ACTIVE TIME
20 MINUTES

TOTAL TIME
45 MINUTES

Beef Barley Soup with Lots of Veggies

PAIR WITH

Potato Rosemary Farls (PAGE 138)

2 Tbsp extra-virgin olive oil
1 large yellow onion, finely chopped
2 large carrots, peeled and chopped
2 celery stalks, thinly sliced
1 large turnip, peeled and chopped
1 Tbsp tomato paste
2 medium garlic cloves, finely chopped
2 tsp chopped fresh thyme
2 tsp chopped fresh rosemary
½ cup [120 ml] red wine (such as a decent Côtes du Rhône)
3 cups [720 ml] beef broth (see page 18)
3 cups [720 ml] chicken broth (see page 17)
1 cup [200 g] pearled barley
1 bay leaf
8 oz [225 g] New York beef strip steak, trimmed and cut into 1-in [2.5-cm] pieces
2 Tbsp red miso
Sea salt
Freshly ground black pepper

1. Heat 1 Tbsp of the olive oil in a large soup pot or Dutch oven over medium-high heat. Add the onion, carrots, celery, and turnip and sauté until the onion is beginning to brown, about 8 minutes. Add the tomato paste, garlic, thyme, and rosemary and sauté until fragrant, about 45 seconds. Add the wine and cook, scraping up any browned bits on the bottom of the pan, until the wine has nearly evaporated, about 1 minute.

2. Add both broths, the barley, and the bay leaf, and cover and bring to a simmer. Reduce the heat to low and simmer gently, stirring occasionally, until the barley is tender but it still has a little pop when bitten into, 20 to 25 minutes.

3. Meanwhile, brown the beef: Adjust the oven rack so it is 6 in [15 cm] below the heating element. Preheat the broiler on high. Line a small baking sheet with aluminum foil.

4. Place the steak on the prepared baking sheet, toss it with the remaining 1 Tbsp olive oil and the miso, and arrange in an even layer. Broil, stirring once, until the meat is browned all over but still pink in the center, about 5 minutes.

5. Transfer the beef and any browned bits and juices from the baking sheet to the pot and cook, uncovered, for 4 minutes. Season with salt and pepper.

6. Ladle the soup into bowls and serve immediately.

GET AHEAD: The soup tastes even better if it is made a day in advance. Store in airtight containers or zip-top plastic freezer bags in the refrigerator for up to 2 days, or in the freezer for up to 3 months.

SERVES

6 TO 8

ACTIVE TIME

12
MINUTES

TOTAL TIME

50
MINUTES

This thick, meaty version of chili comes from Ohio, where it is served over pasta and topped with cheese, chopped onions, and sour cream. It's called four-way because you count one "way" for each additional ingredient, besides the chili. It's a fun approach to serving chili, but what I really love about "Cincy chili" is the deep, woodsy flavors that come from allspice, cinnamon, and a bit of unsweetened cocoa. Talk about beefy!

Since this dish is all about the spices, high-quality chili powder is key for the best results. I recommend Gebhardt's chili powder for bright chile pepper flavor or Penzeys Chili 9000 blend; both are available online. I often crumble corn muffins (see page 167) over the top of the chili in lieu of serving it over pasta, in which case the meal is gluten-free.

Four-Way Cincinnati Chili

PAIR WITH

Gluten-Free Corn Muffins (PAGE 167)
Blue Corn and Maple Skillet Bread (PAGE 152)

1 lb [455 g] 90 percent lean ground chuck beef
2 Tbsp extra-virgin olive oil
1 large yellow onion, finely chopped
3 medium garlic cloves, minced
2 Tbsp chili powder
1 Tbsp ground cumin
1½ tsp ground allspice
1 tsp ground cinnamon
One 28-oz [800-g] can crushed tomatoes with the juice
3 cups [515 g] cooked beans (see page 19) or two 15-oz [425-g] cans pinto or kidney beans, rinsed and drained
2½ cups [600 ml] beef broth (see page 18)
1 Tbsp unsweetened cocoa powder
Sea salt
Freshly ground black pepper
6 oz [170 g] short pasta, such as rotini or elbow macaroni (optional)
1½ cups [120 g] grated Cheddar cheese
½ cup [120 g] sour cream

1. Adjust the oven rack so it is 6 in [15 cm] below the heating element and preheat the broiler on high. Line a rimmed baking sheet with aluminum foil.

2. Spread out the ground beef in an even layer on the prepared baking sheet. Broil, stirring the meat with a spatula once or twice (leave the beef in big chunks for the best texture), until the meat is browned all the way through, about 10 minutes.

3. Meanwhile, start the chili. Heat the oil in a large soup pot or Dutch oven over medium heat. Add all but ½ cup [70 g] of the onion to the pot and sauté until translucent, 5 minutes. Add the garlic, chili powder, cumin, allspice, and cinnamon and cook for 30 seconds, stirring constantly. Add the tomatoes, beans, beef broth, and cocoa powder and stir to combine.

CONTINUED

4. Transfer the beef to the pot with a slotted spoon and discard the fat left on the baking sheet. Reduce the heat to low, cover the pot, and cook, stirring occasionally, until the flavors have melded, 30 to 40 minutes. Season with salt and pepper.

5. While the soup is simmering, cook the pasta according to package instructions, if using.

6. Divide the pasta among six bowls. Top each serving with the chili, reserved onions, cheese, and sour cream. Serve immediately.

GET AHEAD: This freezes well, so you may want to make a double batch. If you do, broil the meat in two batches so that it cooks evenly. Store in airtight containers or zip-top plastic freezer bags in the refrigerator for up to 4 days or in the freezer for up to 3 months.

Hominy (large dried corn kernels) add buttery, popcorn flavor and chewy texture to the tangy Mexican soup known as posole. Instead of browning tough pork shoulder and simmering it for hours, as is traditional, I broil pork tenderloin and add it at the end. A few mild Anaheim chiles added to the broiler pan lend the soup a smoky-spicy base note. You can make this soup vegan by omitting the pork and substituting vegetable broth for the chicken broth. Add a few red potatoes to the pot with the hominy.

Corn tortillas (see page 140) are a traditional accompaniment; the corny flavor of the masa and the hominy work well together.

SERVES

6

ACTIVE TIME

20

MINUTES

TOTAL TIME

40

MINUTES

Pork and Hominy Stew with Roasted Anaheim Chiles

<u>PAIR WITH</u>

Homemade Corn Tortillas (PAGE 140)

1 lb [455 g] pork tenderloin
4 medium green Anaheim chiles
2 Tbsp extra-virgin olive oil
Sea salt
Freshly ground black pepper
1 medium yellow onion, finely chopped
1 large carrot, peeled and thinly sliced
4 medium garlic cloves, minced
2 tsp ground cumin
1 Tbsp chopped fresh oregano,
    or ½ tsp dried Mexican oregano
1½ tsp ground coriander
5 cups [1.2 L] chicken broth
    (see page 17)
One 15-oz [425-g] can
    white hominy, drained
One 12-oz [340-g] can tomatillos,
    drained and chopped
3 Tbsp chopped fresh cilantro
2 Tbsp freshly squeezed lime juice
1 large avocado, pitted, peeled,
    and diced
3 large radishes, thinly sliced

1. Adjust the oven rack so it is 6 in [15 cm] below the heating element and preheat the broiler. Line a rimmed baking sheet with aluminum foil. Trim the tough, silvery white connective tissue (known as silverskin) away from the surface of the tenderloin, if present. Cut the tenderloin into ½-in [12-mm] cubes.

2. Arrange the pork on one side of the prepared baking sheet in a single layer and arrange the chiles on other side. Drizzle the pork with 1 Tbsp of the olive oil, and sprinkle with ½ tsp salt and ½ tsp pepper. Broil, stirring the pork and flipping the chiles once, until the chiles are charred and the pork is lightly browned, about 10 minutes (the pork will finish cooking in the soup).

<u>CONTINUED</u>

3. While the pork and chiles are broiling, heat the remaining 1 Tbsp of olive oil in a large soup pot or Dutch oven over medium-high heat. Add the onion and carrot and sauté until the onion is tender, about 5 minutes. Add the garlic, cumin, oregano, and coriander and cook, stirring constantly, for 30 seconds. Add the broth, hominy, and tomatillos to the pot and stir to combine. Cover, reduce the heat to low, and simmer gently while working on the chiles.

4. When the chiles are ready, pull off the stems and cut the chiles in half lengthwise. Scrape away and discard the skins and seeds. Chop the chiles and add them to the pot, along with the pork and any accumulated juices from the baking sheet.

5. Cover and simmer gently over low heat until the flavors have melded, 10 to 15 minutes. Add the cilantro and lime juice and season with salt and pepper.

6. Serve the soup garnished with the avocado and radishes.

GET AHEAD: Store the cooled soup (without the avocado or radishes) in airtight containers or zip-top plastic freezer bags in the refrigerator for up to 3 days or in the freezer for up to 3 months. Defrost overnight in the refrigerator, and reheat the soup gently or the pork will become tough. The soup may become spicier with time; add additional broth while reheating if necessary.

SERVES

4 TO 6

ACTIVE TIME

20
MINUTES

TOTAL TIME

45
MINUTES

I love gumbo, but I don't love standing in front of a hot pan for 30 minutes, stirring the base flour and oil mixture called "roux." Fortunately, brown roux can be cooked in as little at 6 minutes in the microwave, just enough time to get the Cajun "holy trinity" of onions, peppers, and celery started in the soup pot.

This soup is super-adaptable. I use smoked turkey sausage, but you can substitute 12 oz [340 g] of peeled and deveined shrimp and add them with the okra. Or make the gumbo vegan by substituting a large chopped garnet yam for the sausage and using vegetable broth rather than chicken broth. I prefer frozen or homemade fresh black-eyed peas to mushy canned black-eyed peas. For a complete southern meal, serve this gumbo with the pimento cheese biscuits on page 160, y'all.

Sausage Gumbo

PAIR WITH

Pimento Cheese Drop Biscuits (PAGE 160)

½ cup [70 g] all-purpose flour
½ cup [120 ml] safflower oil
1 large yellow onion, finely chopped
1 large green bell pepper,
    seeded and chopped
3 celery stalks, thinly sliced
7 medium garlic cloves, thinly sliced
1 Tbsp Cajun seasoning
5 cups [1.2 L] chicken or vegetable
    broth (see page 17)
3 cups [540 g] frozen or homemade
    black-eyed peas (see page 19)
12 oz [340 g] smoked turkey or
    pork sausage links, cut into
    bite-size pieces
2 cups [230 g] frozen sliced okra
1 Tbsp apple cider vinegar
2 tsp filé powder
Sea salt
Freshly ground black pepper
Hot sauce, for serving

1. In a microwave-safe glass measuring cup with a 4-cup [960-ml] capacity, whisk together the flour and ¼ cup plus 3 Tbsp [105 ml] of the safflower oil. Microwave on high for 3 minutes, and then use an oven mitt to remove the measuring cup from the microwave and whisk the mixture; be very cautious, because hot roux can cause severe burns. Return the measuring cup to the microwave and cook on high, whisking every minute, until the mixture is the color of an old copper penny, from 3½ to 7 minutes, depending on your microwave.

2. While the roux cooks, heat the remaining 1 Tbsp of the safflower oil in a large soup pot or Dutch oven over medium heat. Add the onion, bell pepper, and celery and sauté, stirring frequently, until the onion is translucent, about 8 minutes. Add the garlic and Cajun seasoning and sauté until fragrant, about 1 minute. Carefully pour the hot roux into the pot and stir to coat the vegetables.

3. Add the chicken broth, black-eyed peas, and sausage to the pot. Cover, bring to a simmer, and reduce the heat to medium-low. Simmer, stirring occasionally, for 10 minutes. Add the okra, reduce the heat to low, and simmer gently, uncovered, until the okra is tender, about 10 minutes.

Remove the pot from the heat, add the vinegar and filé powder, and stir to combine. Season with salt and pepper.

4. Ladle the gumbo into bowls and serve immediately, with a bottle of hot sauce at the ready.

GET AHEAD: Let the roux sit at room temperature in the measuring cup until completely cool, and then pour it into a container with a tight-fitting lid (I use a canning jar). Store in the refrigerator for up to 2 weeks. Before using, whisk the roux thoroughly. The soup can be prepared up to 2 days in advance and reheated gently; add a bit of warm broth if needed to adjust the consistency.

SERVES

4 TO 6

ACTIVE TIME

25

MINUTES

TOTAL TIME

30

MINUTES

This recipe is inspired by the bowls of hearty ramen I slurped in train stations in northern Japan. Sapporo ramen is my favorite style—full of springy ramen noodles, rich and savory red miso broth, buttered corn, boiled eggs, and thin slices of barbecued pork. With a soup spoon in one hand and chopsticks in the other, it's full-contact eating at its best! To make this dish lightning-fast (it's really more about shopping than cooking), I use packaged Chinese char siu (barbecue pork). Look for it in the meat department of grocery stores where precooked ribs are sold. For a more authentic flavor, pick up crisp-skinned barbecued pork (the type hanging among Peking ducks) in Chinese markets.

Barbecue Pork and Miso Ramen

PAIR WITH

Korean Egg Breads (PAGE 162)
Flaky Green Onion Pancakes (PAGE 139)

3 large eggs
8 cups [2 L] chicken broth
  (see page 17)
3 dried shiitake mushrooms
3 slices fresh ginger,
  cut ½ in [12 mm] thick
1¼ lb [570 g] packaged char siu
  (see headnote), thinly sliced
1½ lb [680 g] fresh ramen noodles
2 cups [270 g] frozen corn
2 Tbsp unsalted butter
⅓ cup [80 ml] red miso
2 cups [100 g] bean sprouts,
  loosely packed
4 green onions, thinly sliced
4 to 6 sheets nori seaweed
1 tsp togarashi (Japanese red chile
  seasoning blend) or red chile flakes

1. Bring 8 cups [2 L] water to a boil in a medium saucepan. Gently lower the eggs into the water (the eggs should be completely submerged; add more water if necessary). Reduce the heat to maintain a simmer, and cook for 8 minutes. Remove the eggs from the water and peel them under cold running water. Halve the eggs lengthwise, and set aside.

2. While the water for the eggs is heating up, combine 2 cups [480 ml] of water, the chicken broth, dried mushrooms, and ginger in a large soup pot or Dutch oven and bring to a simmer over high heat. Reduce the heat to low, add the pork, cover, and simmer gently while preparing the other ingredients.

3. Bring a large pot of water to a boil and cook the noodles according to the package instructions. Drain the noodles and divide them among soup bowls.

4. In a large microwave-safe bowl, combine the corn and butter. Microwave on high until the corn is hot to the touch, 3½ minutes. (Alternatively, heat the corn and butter in a small saucepan over medium-low heat.) Set aside.

5. Fish out the mushrooms and ginger from the broth. Thinly slice the mushroom caps and return them to the soup; discard the mushroom stems and ginger. In a small bowl, whisk the miso with 1 cup [240 ml] of the broth and return it to the pot.

6. Ladle the soup over the noodles, arranging the pork and mushrooms on top in neat piles. Arrange small piles of the corn, bean sprouts, and green onions among the pork and mushrooms. Slip a sheet of nori against the side of each bowl, submerging only a small corner of the seaweed in the soup. Place one or two egg halves in the center of each bowl, and sprinkle with the togarashi. Serve immediately.

GET AHEAD: The broth (with the mushrooms, ginger, and pork in it) can be stored in the refrigerator for up to 2 days. Before serving, cook the eggs and noodles, and microwave the frozen corn with the butter. Reheat the broth over medium-low heat and serve as directed.

SERVES

4 TO 6

ACTIVE TIME

15

MINUTES

TOTAL TIME

45

MINUTES

I've sampled the dishes from street-food stands all over Jamaica, and my hands down favorite dish is their thick, spicy "brown stew." The hearty stew is full of whatever local vegetables are around and includes some sort of meat—chicken or goat being the most common. I opt for spice-coated pork tenderloin here. The fruity heat of habanero chile is pronounced, so if your family isn't fond of spicy food, omit the chile and serve habanero hot sauce on the side. The subtle sweetness of the corn and maple skillet bread on page 152 plays nicely with the spice here.

Jamaican Pork and Sweet Potato Stew

<u>PAIR WITH</u>

Blue Corn and Maple Skillet Bread (PAGE 152)

2 Tbsp extra-virgin olive oil
1 medium yellow onion, finely chopped
1 red bell pepper, seeded and chopped
1 large carrot, peeled and chopped
4 medium garlic cloves, minced
1 Tbsp minced fresh ginger
1 Tbsp fresh chopped thyme
½ tsp finely chopped habanero chile,
    or more to taste
2 Tbsp tomato paste
6 cups [1.4 L] chicken broth
    (see page 17)
One 1¼-lb [570-g] sweet potato or
    garnet yam, peeled and cut into
    ½-in [12-mm] chunks
2 Tbsp Worcestershire sauce
1¼ lb [570 g] pork tenderloin, trimmed
    and cut into ½-in [12-mm] cubes
    (see trimming instructions on
    page 113)
1 Tbsp all-purpose flour
2 tsp brown sugar
1¼ tsp ground allspice
½ tsp ground cinnamon
½ tsp freshly ground black pepper
½ tsp sea salt
1 to 2 Tbsp freshly squeezed lime juice
Soy sauce, for seasoning

1. Adjust the oven rack so it is 6 in [15 cm] below the heating element and preheat the broiler. Line a baking sheet with aluminum foil.

2. Heat 1 Tbsp of the oil in a large soup pot or Dutch oven over medium-high heat. Add the onion, bell pepper, and carrot and sauté until the onion is translucent, about 5 minutes. Add the garlic, ginger, thyme, and habanero and cook for 1 minute, stirring constantly. Add the tomato paste and stir to coat the vegetables. Add the chicken broth, sweet potato, and Worcestershire. Bring to a simmer over medium-high heat, reduce the heat to low, and simmer, uncovered, stirring occasionally, until the sweet potato is tender, about 15 minutes.

3. While the soup is simmering, place the pork on the prepared baking sheet and toss with the remaining 1 Tbsp olive oil. Sprinkle the meat with the flour, brown sugar, allspice, cinnamon, pepper, and salt and toss to coat. Arrange the meat in a single layer and broil, without stirring, until the meat is browned on one side, 4 to 5 minutes (the pork will finish cooking in the soup).

4. Transfer the pork and drippings from the baking sheet to the pot. Simmer gently, uncovered, stirring occasionally, until the flavors have melded and the soup has thickened a bit, about 10 minutes more. If you'd like the soup to be still thicker, use a potato masher to mash some of the sweet potato. Season the soup with the lime juice and soy sauce.

5. Ladle the stew into bowls and serve immediately.

GET AHEAD: This recipe doubles easily, tastes better the next day, and freezes well. Go easy on the habanero; just ½ of the finely chopped chile will be plenty, as the stew will become spicier the next day. Store in airtight containers or zip-top plastic freezer bags in the refrigerator for up to 4 days or the freezer for up to 3 months.

SERVES

4 TO 6

ACTIVE TIME

25

MINUTES

TOTAL TIME

45

MINUTES

Called harira *in Morocco, this hearty lamb, garbanzo bean, and lentil soup is traditionally served in the evening, after everyone has fasted all day during the holy month of Ramadan. The soup is seasoned with harissa, a fiery red-chile-and-spice paste found in colorful tubes and small cans in grocery stores and online. The spiciness of harissa varies from brand to brand; taste it first and add it to the soup according to your heat tolerance. Though this soup is usually made with chunks of lamb, I prefer quick-cooking, bite-size lamb meatballs instead. You can make the soup vegan by omitting the meat altogether and using vegetable broth; it's equally delicious. For gluten-free* harira, *omit the couscous.*

Lamb Meatball, Garbanzo Bean, Lentil, and Tomato Soup

PAIR WITH

Quick Flatbread with Dukkah (PAGE 135)

1 lb [455 g] ground lamb
½ Tbsp harissa, plus extra for
    seasoning the soup
Sea salt
Freshly ground black pepper
2 Tbsp extra-virgin olive oil
1 large yellow onion, finely chopped
2 medium carrots, peeled and thinly
    sliced into coins ¼ in [6 mm] thick
2 Tbsp minced fresh ginger
2 large garlic cloves, minced
1 tsp ground cumin
½ tsp ground cinnamon
6 cups [1.4 L] chicken or vegetable
    broth (see page 17)
1½ cups [255 g] cooked garbanzo
    beans (see page 19), or one 15-oz
    [425-g] can garbanzo beans,
    rinsed and drained
1½ cups [370 g] diced tomatoes
    in purée
½ cup [85 g] brown lentils,
    picked over and rinsed

2 medium medjool dates,
    pitted and chopped
3 Tbsp couscous
¼ cup [7 g] chopped fresh cilantro
2 Tbsp freshly squeezed lemon juice

1. Preheat the oven to 425°F [220°C]. Line a rimmed baking sheet with parchment paper or aluminum foil.

2. In a large bowl, mix the lamb with the ½ Tbsp of harissa, ¾ tsp salt, and ½ tsp pepper and blend thoroughly. Pinch off little dabs of the meat (about 1 Tbsp each) and place them on the prepared baking sheet. (There's no need to roll them into perfect spheres unless you are so inclined.) Bake, stirring once, until the meatballs are no longer pink in the center, about 10 minutes. Drain off and discard the fat.

CONTINUED

3. Meanwhile, heat the olive oil in a large soup pot or Dutch oven over medium heat. Add the onion and carrots and sauté, stirring frequently, until the onion is translucent, about 5 minutes. Add the ginger, garlic, cumin, and cinnamon and cook, stirring constantly, until fragrant, about 45 seconds. Add more harissa to taste and stir to combine.

4. Add the chicken broth, garbanzo beans, tomatoes, and lentils to the pot. Cover and bring to a boil over medium-high heat. Reduce the heat to medium-low and simmer, stirring occasionally, until the lentils are almost tender, about 15 minutes. Add the meatballs, dates, couscous, and cilantro and simmer, uncovered, until the couscous is tender and the soup has thickened slightly, about 5 minutes. Add the lemon juice and season with salt and pepper, adding more harissa if desired.

5. Ladle the soup into bowls and serve immediately.

GET AHEAD: The lamb meatballs can be made and stored in the refrigerator up to 3 days. The entire soup can be stored in airtight containers or zip-top plastic freezer bags in the refrigerator for up to 2 days or in the freezer for up to 3 months. The soup will thicken upon standing; add more broth to the soup when reheating leftovers, if desired.

Irish stew is traditionally made with tough cuts of lamb or mutton, simmered for hours to tenderize them. I expedite things by using tender lamb shoulder chops or beef sirloin (or a mix of the two), and use demiglace concentrate so the stew tastes like it's been bubbling away on the stove for hours. The entire enterprise takes under an hour, but it tastes like the best stews I've enjoyed in country pubs in Ireland. There the stew is never served without a hearty slab of soda bread (see page 149) for sopping up the thick broth, so I follow suit at home.

SERVES
6

ACTIVE TIME
15
MINUTES

TOTAL TIME
45
MINUTES

Fast Irish Stew

PAIR WITH

Mini–Irish Soda Breads (PAGE 149)
Potato Rosemary Farls (PAGE 138)

2¼ lb [1 kg] lamb shoulder blade chops, or 2 lb [910 g] beef sirloin steak
Sea salt
Freshly ground black pepper
3 Tbsp extra-virgin olive oil
1 medium yellow onion, chopped
2 medium carrots, peeled and thinly sliced into coins
1 Tbsp finely chopped fresh thyme
¼ cup [35 g] all-purpose flour
1 cup [240 ml] stout beer
2 Tbsp demiglace concentrate (see Flavor Toolbox, page 12)
1 lb [455g] Yukon Gold potatoes (2 large), unpeeled, cut into chunks ½ in [12 mm] thick
2 Tbsp tomato paste
1 Tbsp Worcestershire sauce
1 bay leaf

1. Adjust the oven rack so it is 6 in [15 cm] below the heating element and preheat the broiler. Line a rimmed baking sheet with aluminum foil.

2. If using lamb, trim the meat away from the bones and cut it into ½-in [12-mm] pieces, discarding any hard white fat and reserving the bones. If using the beef, trim off the fat and cut into pieces of the same size. Place the lamb and lamb bones or the beef on the prepared baking sheet, season generously with salt and pepper, and drizzle with 1 Tbsp of the olive oil. Toss to coat the meat and bones and spread them out in an even layer on the pan. Broil, stirring once, until the meat is well browned but still medium-rare to rare in the center, about 5 minutes.

CONTINUED

3. While the meat is cooking, heat the remaining 2 Tbsp of olive oil in a large soup pot or Dutch oven over medium heat. Add the onion, carrots, and thyme and sauté until the onion is translucent, about 4 minutes. Sprinkle the flour over the vegetables and cook, stirring frequently, for 1 minute. Add the beer and cook for 1 minute, scraping up the browned bits on the bottom of the pan. Add 3 cups [720 ml] hot water, the demi-glace concentrate, potatoes, tomato paste, Worcestershire, and bay leaf (and the lamb bones, if using) and bring to a simmer. Cover partially, reduce the heat to low, and cook, stirring frequently, until the potatoes are just tender, about 15 minutes.

4. Add the broiled meat and any accumulated juices to the pot. Cook, uncovered, for 10 minutes; do not boil, or the meat will become tough. Remove and discard the bones and bay leaf. Season with salt and pepper.

5. Divide the soup among individual bowls and serve immediately.

GET AHEAD: This stew freezes well, so you may want to make a double batch. If you do, broil the meat in two batches so that it cooks evenly. Store the cooled stew in airtight containers or zip-top plastic freezer bags in the refrigerator for up to 4 days, or in the freezer for up to 3 months. Defrost the frozen stew overnight in the refrigerator and reheat gently.

CHAPTER 3

Breads to Match

Breads

I've saved the best for last. In the following pages you'll find twenty-five bread recipes that partner with the preceding soups to make a complete meal. I start with thirteen tips and some troubleshooting to up your baking game. Then we'll explore the fastest breads of all, the flat ones. From a delightfully easy-to-work-with, yogurt-based dough in Quick Flatbread with Three Toppings (page 135) to the soulful goodness of Homemade Corn Tortillas (page 140), flat is the new black.

You don't have to get out the rolling pin to make great bread, though. There's a range of savory soda breads and skillet breads, such as Blue Corn and Maple Skillet Bread (page 152) and Spinach and Sun-Dried Tomato Scones (page 154), which are simple mix-and-go recipes. There are also savory muffins and one-bowl biscuits like Quinoa, Apple, and Cheddar Muffins (page 171), Everything Rye Muffins (page 170), and Pimento Cheese Drop Biscuits (page 160) that are so easy to make, even the most baking-phobic cook can master them with ease.

For those of you who are veteran bakers, I'm eager to show you some new twists on old familiar forms and some very interesting breads that use ancient grains like teff flour *injera* (see page 145), and unusual cooking methods like Malaysian curry net breads (see page 147). In this chapter there is a bread for every soup and a bread for every type of baker.

A Baker's Dozen—13 Tips for the Best Breads

1. **GET FRESH.** Most of the breads in this book use chemical leavening (baking soda or baking powder) for lift, with a few yeasty exceptions. Like other pantry items, chemical leaveners don't keep their freshness indefinitely. Mark a newly opened container of leavener with the date and discard it after 6 months. Yeast lasts 4 months when stored in the freezer.

2. **FAT IS WHERE THE FLAVOR IS.** Fat gives quick baked goods a lot of flavor, so splurge a little; you'll taste the difference. I use European-style cultured butter, fancy extra-virgin olive oil, and artisan cheeses for the recipes in the book. You should, too.

3. **MAKE YOUR OWN BUTTERMILK.** The acidity in buttermilk helps activate baking powder and baking soda, which is why it's included in many recipes in this book. Buttermilk also lends bread tenderness and a tasty tang, but it's not something most of us have around all the time. To make your own faux buttermilk, mix 1 cup [240 ml] milk with 1 Tbsp lemon juice and set aside for 5 minutes to thicken. Use immediately.

4. **FREEZE WHOLE-GRAIN FLOURS.** I use white whole-wheat flour and other whole-grain flours quite a bit in this book, for both flavor and fiber. Whole-grain flour is made from grinding the entire grain, including the high-fat germ. These fats can go rancid at room temperature and give baked goods an off flavor. That's why I keep my whole-grain flours in airtight containers in the freezer. They last up to 6 months.

5. **WEIGH DRY INGREDIENTS.** Measuring by volume with measuring cups is very inaccurate—1 cup of flour can weigh anywhere from 5 to 7 oz [140 to 200 g], depending on how you put the flour in the cup and how aerated the flour is. For the best results, get a basic digital scale with a gram setting. Weighing is not only more accurate but also faster, and it dirties fewer dishes! A scale in the kitchen is handy for weighing vegetables and meats, too.

6. **WORK LEFT TO RIGHT.** The best pastry chef I know assembles all the ingredients to the left of the mixing bowl before she starts. As she adds each ingredient, she puts the ingredient down on the right side of the bowl. That way, she never wonders whether she remembered the salt, baking powder, or cinnamon; she's got visual notes.

7. **DON'T OVERMIX.** Most of the breads in this book are "short doughs"; that is, they don't require a lot of kneading. Instead, they use fat to keep the gluten strands in the dough short, which gives them a tender and rich texture—think scones and muffins. Once you add the liquid ingredients to the dry ingredients, stir only to moisten. Unless otherwise noted, be gentle and handle dough only as much as you have to in order to get the job done.

8. **USE ICE-CREAM AND COOKIE-DOUGH SCOOPS.** Pastry chefs use ice-cream and cookie-dough scoops to portion and transfer batter or dough quickly and neatly to baking sheets and muffin tins.

<u>CONTINUED</u>

9. **GOOD BAKING SHEETS ARE YOUR BESTIES.** These workhorses of the kitchen are not all created equal. Standard thin baking sheets warp and deliver uneven baking (and even burning). Take a trip to a restaurant supply store and buy shiny "half sheet trays," which measure 15 by 18 in [38 by 46 cm], with a 1-in [2.5-cm] rim. You'll pay less than you would at fancy kitchen stores and they'll last a lifetime. Opt for light-colored baking sheets in lieu of darker ones, which retain more heat and can cause breads to brown too quickly.

10. **KNOW THY OVEN.** Ovens can become decalibrated over time. Buy a small, inexpensive oven thermometer and place it in the center of your oven from time to time. Once the oven is preheated, cross-check the temperature your oven says it's reached with the thermometer in the oven. Adjust accordingly.

11. **DON'T TRUST THE TIMER.** I offer both time and doneness cues in the bread recipes in this book, because every oven is different. The baking times are a guideline, but checking the doneness by inserting a skewer into the bread or using the visuals provided is key to determining doneness. Keep an eye on your bread(s) and you will be met with success.

12. **INDIVIDUALLY QUICK-FREEZE.** When freezing small breads like scones and biscuits for future baking, place them on a baking sheet or plate until solid. Then transfer them to a space-saving zip-top plastic freezer bag. This way, they will be easy to separate when it's time to bake.

13. **COOL IT.** I know you are in a hurry, but it's best to let the quick breads, biscuits, and muffins in this book cool on a wire rack for a few ticks before serving them. It will deepen their flavor and improve their texture. Conversely, flatbreads (tortillas, pancakes, and so on) are best served immediately, as indicated in the recipes.

Troubleshooting Breads

PROBLEM: "My bread/muffins are too dense."

SOLUTION: How old is your leavening? Baking soda, baking powder, and yeast all have a shelf life. Dense bread can also be a sign of too much flour in the dough. When you are using more than 3 Tbsp of a dry ingredient, weigh it instead of using a measuring cup.

PROBLEM: "My muffins/biscuits are rubbery and tough."

SOLUTION: Don't overmix muffin, biscuit, scone, or bread batter. Stir gently until there are no traces of dry flour and the dry ingredients are just moistened. Overmixing yields tough bread.

PROBLEM: "My bread fell flat."

SOLUTION: You may be opening the oven door too often to check your breads. This can cause the oven temperature to drop significantly, which may interfere with the rising of your breads. Unless you're in the last few minutes of the suggested baking time, or need to rotate the baking pan, keep the oven door closed and look through the oven window; that's what it's for.

PROBLEM: "My muffins have sweaty bottoms."

SOLUTION: Let muffins cool in the pan for no more than 10 minutes before transferring them to a cooling rack. Over time, the steam has nowhere to go but the bottom of the baking tin, which causes condensation and soggy muffin bottoms.

Flatbreads

This flatbread dough is leavened with baking powder and enriched with olive oil and full-fat yogurt. The yogurt makes it a dream to knead and roll out, and if the stars all align correctly, you'll end up with a great big puffed-up bread that resembles a pita on steroids. Place it on a big platter in the center of the table, and invite your family to tear off pieces to dip into soup, surrounded by billows of steam escaping from the bread.

This flatbread is great simply brushed with good extra-virgin olive oil and sprinkled with sea salt (it's more likely to puff up dramatically prepared this way). But I also love to dress it up a bit with anchovy-garlic-herb butter; or sprinkle it with the beguiling blend of nuts, seeds, and spices called dukkah; or give it an Italian spin with a bit of fresh sheep's milk cheese and olives. It all depends on the soup I'm going to serve it with. This bread really is best straight out of the oven, so have your soup ready to go before you slip the flatbread into the oven.

Quick Flatbread with Three Toppings

PAIR WITH

Dukkah: Persian Yogurt, Lentil, and Bulgur Soup with Browned Herb Butter (PAGE 62)
Olive and Pecorino: Broken Pasta and Bean Soup (PAGE 71)
Anchovy Butter: Crab, Halibut, and Squid Cioppino (PAGE 78)

MAKES

1

LARGE FLATBREAD

SERVES

4 TO 6

ACTIVE TIME

15

MINUTES

TOTAL TIME

40

MINUTES

1¼ cups [175 g] all-purpose flour, plus more as needed
½ cup [70 g] whole-wheat flour
¾ tsp baking powder
½ tsp sea salt
1 Tbsp extra-virgin olive oil
1 cup [240 g] full-fat plain Greek yogurt
2 Tbsp coarse cornmeal
Dukkah, Olive and Pecorino Topping, or Anchovy-Garlic Butter (see page 137; optional)

1. Place a pizza stone or heavy, rimless baking sheet in the center of the oven and preheat to 450°F [230°C].

2. In a large bowl, whisk together both flours, the baking powder, and salt. Add the olive oil and stir with your fingers until the mixture looks like crumbly granola. Add the yogurt and stir with a wooden spoon until the dough comes together. Transfer the dough to a lightly floured surface and knead for 3 minutes, or until smooth, adding flour as needed to keep the dough from sticking. (Alternatively, mix and knead in a stand mixer fitted with a dough hook or a food processor fitted with the dough blade.)

CONTINUED

3. Roll out the dough into a 15-in [38-cm] round. No need to be perfect here; just a generally circular shape is fine. Sprinkle a pizza peel or the back of a baking sheet with the cornmeal. Place the dough on the peel (it's fine if it's hanging off the edges just a little). Top with 3 Tbsp of the dukkah, or all of the olive and pecorino topping, if using (but hold off on the anchovy-garlic butter option). Gently press the topping into the dough. Open the oven door and slide the flatbread onto the preheated pizza stone or baking sheet with a decisive jerking motion. Bake until the bread is puffed and golden brown, about 10 minutes. Brush the bread with the anchovy-garlic butter, if using.

4. Transfer the flatbread to a large platter and place in the center of the table immediately. Serve family style, inviting diners to tear off pieces of the bread with their fingers, or cut into wedges before serving.

Dukkah

MAKES 1 CUP [140 G], ENOUGH FOR 5 FLATBREADS

Toast 2 Tbsp coriander seeds and 2 Tbsp cumin seeds in a dry sauté pan over medium-low heat until aromatic, about 3 minutes. Grind the spices with a mortar and pestle or in a clean spice grinder. Transfer to a small bowl and add ½ cup [70 g] toasted and finely chopped hazelnuts, ¼ cup [35 g] toasted sesame seeds, 1 tsp dried marjoram, 1 tsp dried mint, ¾ tsp sea salt, and ¾ tsp freshly ground pepper. Store in an airtight container at room temperature for up to 2 weeks.

Olive and Pecorino Topping

MAKES ¾ CUP [110 G], ENOUGH FOR 1 FLATBREAD

In a small bowl, combine ¼ cup [40 g] chopped pitted kalamata olives with ¾ cup [70 g] grated pecorino fresco (or other mild, semi-firm sheep's milk cheese), and 2 Tbsp chopped fresh basil leaves. Use immediately.

Anchovy-Garlic Butter

MAKES ⅓ CUP [80 G], ENOUGH FOR 1 FLATBREAD

On a cutting board, mound 1½ Tbsp fresh Italian parsley leaves, 1 Tbsp fresh dill, 2 oil-packed anchovies, ½ small peeled garlic clove, and ¾ tsp finely grated lemon zest and work with a chef's knife until the garlic is very finely chopped. Transfer the herb mixture to a small bowl and stir in 2 tbsp [30 g] room-temperature unsalted butter and ½ tsp freshly squeezed lemon juice. Season with sea salt and freshly ground black pepper. Store in an airtight container in the refrigerator for up to 1 week.

MAKES

8

FARLS

SERVES

4 TO 8

ACTIVE TIME

15

MINUTES

TOTAL TIME

15

MINUTES

A farl is a delicious cross between a potato cake and a scone. They're served in Northern Ireland as part of their signature "Ulster fry" breakfasts, but I think they're great served at supper with beef barley soup or lamb stew. Farl means "fourth," so called because the thick pancake is panfried and cut into quarters for serving. I prefer to cut the dough into smaller, thicker eighths while still raw and then panfry them individually; they cook more quickly and brown more evenly this way.

Potato Rosemary Farls

PAIR WITH

Beef Barley Soup with Lots of Veggies (PAGE 109)
Fast Irish Stew (PAGE 125)

2 cups [455 g] leftover mashed
    potatoes or packaged
    prepared mashed potatoes
3 Tbsp unsalted butter,
    at room temperature
1 tsp chopped fresh rosemary
½ tsp sea salt
¼ tsp freshly ground black pepper
⅛ tsp baking soda
About ½ cup [70 g] all-purpose flour

1. Place the mashed potatoes in a large bowl and add 1 Tbsp of the butter, the rosemary, salt, pepper, and baking soda. Stir in enough of the flour to make a soft, slightly sticky dough; do not overmix.

2. Turn the dough out onto a well-floured surface and pat it into a round ½ in [12 mm] thick and about 9 in [23 cm] in diameter. Cut the round into 8 equal wedges.

3. Melt the remaining 2 tablespoons butter in a large cast-iron skillet or sauté pan over medium heat. Using an offset spatula dipped in flour, transfer the dough wedges to the skillet and cook until browned and crisp, about 5 minutes per side.

4. Serve the farls warm.

GET AHEAD: Let the farls cool completely, wrap them in foil, and refrigerate for up to 4 days. Reheat in a large dry skillet over medium-low heat until heated through, 10 minutes.

This is possibly the most fiddly bread in this book, but it's also the most fun. The pancakes have delicious, flaky layers and are ideal for soups with an Asian bent. The lightly charred flavor means it's great with similarly smoky soups, too.

Flaky Green Onion Pancakes

PAIR WITH

Winter Melon Soup with Smoky Ham (PAGE 45)
Spice-Roasted Butternut Squash Soup with Bacon
Crumbles (PAGE 42)

MAKES

2

PANCAKES

SERVES

4 TO 6

ACTIVE TIME

30

MINUTES

TOTAL TIME

40

MINUTES

1 cup [140 g] all-purpose flour
¼ tsp sea salt
¼ cup plus 1½ tsp [70 ml]
    toasted sesame oil
½ cup [120 ml] boiling water
2 green onions, finely chopped

1. In a large bowl, whisk together the flour and salt. Add 1½ tsp of the sesame oil and the boiling water and stir until the mixture comes together into a shaggy dough. Turn the dough out onto a lightly floured surface and knead until smooth and no longer pockmarked, about 2 minutes. Cover the dough with plastic wrap and set it aside for 10 minutes. Divide into two equal pieces.

2. On a lightly floured surface, roll one of the pieces of dough into a 12-in [30.5-cm] round, rotating the dough occasionally to make sure it's not sticking to the work surface.

3. Brush the pancake with 2 tsp of the remaining sesame oil, leaving a ½-in [12-mm] border without oil around the edges. Sprinkle the pancake with half of the green onions. Starting with the edge closest to you, roll up the pancake into a tight cylinder. Pinch the ends together to seal in the green onions, and pull on the ends gently to elongate the cylinder until it is about 14 in [35.5 cm] long. Coil the cylinder into a tight spiral (it will look like a little snail shell on its side). Cover the dough loosely with plastic wrap and set aside. Repeat the process with the remaining piece of dough.

4. Heat a 12- to 14-in [30.5- to 35.5-cm] skillet (preferably cast-iron) over medium heat. While the skillet heats, roll out the pancakes a final time: With the palm of your hand, press down on one of the coils to flatten it. Roll the dough into a 10-in [25-cm] pancake. Place the pancake in the skillet and cook until golden brown with a few dark brown spots, 2 to 3 minutes per side. Reduce the heat if the pancake begins to brown too quickly and press with a spatula on any areas that remain uncooked (they will be yellowish instead of opaque white or golden brown). Cut the pancake into wedges, stack the wedges, and wrap tightly in foil to keep them warm. Repeat the process with the other coil of dough.

5. Serve the pancakes warm.

GET AHEAD: Leftovers can be kept tightly wrapped in foil in the refrigerator for up to 2 days. To reheat, return the wedges to a skillet set over medium heat and cook until warm and pliable. If they are on the dry side, flick them with a little cold water before reheating.

SERVES

4 TO **6**

ACTIVE TIME

20

MINUTES

TOTAL TIME

20

MINUTES

Soft, warm, and full of corn flavor, homemade tortillas are worth the small amount of effort they require. Though you can easily roll the dough out between sheets of plastic wrap, investing in a tortilla press makes the job a breeze. Look for metal tortilla presses at Latin American grocery stores and kitchenware shops. Serve these tortillas alongside soups with zesty, spicy flavors, such as a posole (see page 113).

Homemade Corn Tortillas

PAIR WITH

Pork and Hominy Stew with Roasted Anaheim Chiles (PAGE 113)
Mexican Chicken Noodle Soup (PAGE 100)

1½ cups [180 g] masa harina (look for "para hacer tortillas"—"for making tortillas"—on the label)
¼ tsp sea salt
2 Tbsp safflower oil or melted coconut oil

1. In a large bowl, combine the masa harina and salt. Add the safflower oil and mix with a fork until crumbly looking. Gradually add 1 cup [240 ml] warm water and stir until smooth. Knead and squish with your fingers in the bowl until smooth, about 1 minute.

2. Heat a large cast-iron frying pan or griddle over medium-high heat. Meanwhile, pinch off a golf ball–size piece of dough and roll it into a smooth ball. Place the ball between pieces of plastic wrap and put it in a tortilla press. Press down firmly, open the press; turn the tortilla, in the plastic wrap, a quarter turn and press again. Repeat with one more quarter turn to press the tortilla evenly into a 5½- to 6-in [14- to 15-cm] round.

3. Open the press, and quickly peel off the top piece of plastic. Pull the bottom piece of plastic wrap, with the tortilla on it, onto your palm, plastic-side down. (If the first tortilla is fighting you and seems sticky and difficult to release from the plastic, knead a bit of masa harina into the big ball of dough and try again.)

4. Quickly flip the tortilla into the pan, releasing it from the plastic, and cook until it releases from the pan easily and has browned spots, about 1½ minutes. Flip the tortilla with a spatula and cook, pressing with the spatula from time to time, until the tortilla is browned, 1 minute. (Adjust the heat as necessary so that the tortillas cook completely without burning around the edges.) You should be able to cook a few tortillas at a time. Wrap the cooked tortillas in a clean kitchen towel or in aluminum foil to keep them warm as you repeat the process with the remaining dough.

5. Serve the warm tortillas immediately.

GET AHEAD: I often make a double batch and bank some of these for later. Let the tortillas cool completely, wrap in foil, and then stuff into a zip-top plastic freezer bag and store in the freezer for up to 3 months. To reheat, wrap the frozen tortillas in a double layer of damp paper towels and microwave them on high until hot, about 1 minute. Serve immediately; they will become tough when they completely cool.

Another option for leftover tortillas is to sandwich a sprinkle of grated cheese between two defrosted tortillas and toast them in a buttered skillet over medium heat until the cheese has melted and the tortillas are crisp around the edges, about 2 minutes per side.

MAKES

FOCACCIA

SERVES

4 TO 6

ACTIVE TIME

10
MINUTES

TOTAL TIME

MINUTES

This flatbread is ideal for pairing with soup. The crispy olive oil–coated crust keeps the bread from getting too soggy when you dip it into soup, so it stands up to multiple dips. This recipe is best when made with Fresh-and-Fast Olive Oil Bread Dough; the dough just needs to be mixed, and a quick 30-minute rise follows on the baking sheet. If you're in a real hurry, substitute fresh pizza dough from the grocery store; look for it in paper bags in the refrigerated section. This focaccia has soft, golden brown garlic cloves baked into the dough. If you don't have the time to peel garlic and cook it in olive oil for a few minutes, your best bet is the roasted garlic available in some gourmet olive bars, where antipasti are sold.

This is my go-to bread for brothy Italian soups.

Roasted Garlic Focaccia

PAIR WITH

Creamy Cannellini Bean Soup with Gremolata (PAGE 56)
Farro Minestrone (PAGE 66)

½ cup [120 ml] plus 1 Tbsp
   extra-virgin olive oil
1 Tbsp medium cornmeal
1 recipe Fresh-and-Fast Olive Oil
   Bread Dough (page 20), or 1 lb
   [455 g] packaged fresh pizza dough
½ cup [80 g] medium garlic cloves,
   peeled
1 tsp coarse sea salt

1. Preheat the oven to 450°F [230°C]. Brush a 10-by-15-in [25-by-38-cm] baking sheet with 1 Tbsp of the olive oil and sprinkle evenly with the cornmeal.

2. Place the dough on the prepared baking sheet and push and stretch with your fingertips into a rectangle roughly 9 by 12 in [23 by 30.5 cm] and about ½ in [12 mm] thick. If the dough snaps back as you stretch it, let it rest for a few minutes and try again. Cover the dough loosely with plastic wrap and set aside in a warm place until risen and puffy, about 30 minutes.

3. Meanwhile, combine the remaining ½ cup [120 ml] olive oil and the garlic cloves in a small saucepan and bring to a simmer over medium-low heat. Cook, stirring frequently, until the garlic is softened and light golden brown, about 5 minutes. Remove the pan from the heat and use a fork to remove the garlic from the oil. Set aside the oil and the garlic.

4. When the dough has finished rising, uncover it and press the garlic cloves gently into the dough all over. Drizzle about half of the reserved olive oil over the dough and sprinkle with the salt. (Save the remaining oil for another use in an airtight container in the refrigerator for up to 2 weeks.)

5. Bake the focaccia until golden brown and crisp, 10 to 15 minutes. Cut into squares or wedges and serve warm.

GET AHEAD: Cool the focaccia, wrap tightly in foil, and store in the refrigerator for up to 2 days. Reheat the bread, wrapped in foil, in a 400°F [200°C] oven until warm, 15 minutes.

If using frozen Fresh-and-Fast Olive Oil Bread Dough (page 20), defrost it overnight in the refrigerator or at room temperature for 4 to 6 hours before proceeding with the recipe.

A cross between flaky biscuits and crunchy saltine crackers, these little goodies offer crispy layers on the outside and a little softness on the inside, with a yeasty, hoppy flavor that reminds me of sourdough bread. With that sort of flavor profile and texture, they are just begging to be dunked into a rich chowder.

Pilot Biscuits

PAIR WITH

Creamy New England–Style Clam Chowder (PAGE 85)
Smoked Salmon and Celery Root Chowder (PAGE 86)

MAKES ABOUT **50** BISCUITS

SERVES **6**

ACTIVE TIME **15** MINUTES

TOTAL TIME **40** MINUTES

5 Tbsp [75 g] cold unsalted butter,
   plus 2 Tbsp butter, melted
2¼ cups [315 g] all-purpose flour
1 Tbsp nutritional yeast
1½ tsp baking powder
1 tsp sea salt
1 cup [240 ml] craft lager beer

1. Preheat the oven to 425°F [220°C]. Line two baking sheets with parchment paper.

2. Cut the cold butter into ¼-in [6-mm] dice and place in the freezer to keep as cold as possible.

3. In a food processor, pulse the flour, nutritional yeast, baking powder, and salt briefly until combined. Add the cold butter and pulse until it is in tiny bits. Add the beer and pulse until just combined; the mixture will be quite sticky. (Alternatively, in a large bowl, whisk the dry ingredients together and cut in the butter with a pastry blender. Stir in the beer with a wooden spoon.)

4. Turn the dough out onto a generously floured work surface and pat into a square 1 in [2.5 cm] thick. Dust the top of the dough with more flour and roll it out into a 15-by-10-in [38-by-25-cm] rectangle. Brush off any excess flour. Brush the dough with the melted butter and letter-fold the dough: bring the short edge of the dough up and over to cover two-thirds of the dough. Fold the opposite short end up and over the double layers of dough to create a skinny rectangle. Dust the top of the dough with flour and roll it out into a roughly 15-by-10-in [38-by-25-cm] rectangle that is about ¼ in [6 mm] thick. (Don't fret if the dough isn't perfectly rectangular.)

5. Using a pastry wheel or pizza cutter, cut off the untidy edges of the dough so it is an even rectangle, and set aside the scraps. Cut the rectangle into strips 2 in [5 cm] wide. Transfer the strips to one of the prepared baking sheets and cut crosswise into 2-in [5-cm] squares. Prick each biscuit twice with a fork. Bake, rotating the baking sheet once, until the biscuits are golden brown and crisp, 15 to 18 minutes.

6. While the first batch bakes, gather up the scraps and repeat the rolling, cutting, and baking.

7. Serve the biscuits warm.

GET AHEAD: Place the unbaked biscuit squares on a parchment-lined plate in the freezer and freeze until solid. Transfer the biscuits to a zip-top plastic freezer bag and freeze for up to 3 months. Bake the frozen biscuits at 400°F [200°C] until golden brown and crisp on the outside, 20 to 25 minutes.

MAKES

72

BREADSTICKS

SERVES

6 TO 8

ACTIVE TIME

15

MINUTES

TOTAL TIME

30

MINUTES

I learned to make these crispy corkscrew breadsticks at the apron strings of a chef in Barbaresco, Italy. Though these breadsticks, called grissini *in Italian, are usually served with appetizer platters, I like to balance the delicate twigs on the edge of soup bowls or stand them upright in a tall glass.*

I keep the flavors simple here, but my friend and expert recipe tester Jacki loves them sprinkled with fried shallots (see Flavor Toolbox, page 14). You could also give them your own twist with a sprinkle of finely grated Parmigiano-Reggiano cheese, poppy seeds, smoked paprika, or crumbled nori seaweed sheets. Sprinkle your chosen flavoring on the rolled-out dough and roll over it gently with a rolling pin before you cut the dough into strips.

Thin and Crispy Breadsticks

PAIR WITH

Blender Gazpacho (PAGE 29)
Spice-Roasted Butternut Squash Soup with Bacon Crumbles (PAGE 42)

1 recipe Fresh-and-Fast Olive Oil Bread Dough (page 20), or 1 lb [455 g] packaged fresh pizza dough
Olive oil spray, for misting
Sea salt

1. Preheat the oven to 375°F [190°C]. Line two baking sheets with parchment paper.

2. Divide the dough in half. On a lightly floured work surface, roll out one half of the dough, picking up the dough and rotating it to make sure it's not sticking, until it is in a roughly 10-by-12-in [25-by-30.5-cm] rectangular shape about ⅛ in [4 mm] thick. If the dough springs back, let it rest for 5 minutes before continuing. (Keep the other half of the dough covered with plastic wrap so it won't dry out.)

3. Sprinkle the dough with additional seasonings (see headnote for ideas), if using. Roll over the seasonings with a rolling pin once to help them adhere to the dough. Using a pastry wheel or pizza cutter, cut the dough into strips ¼ in [8 mm] thick. Transfer the strips to the prepared baking sheets and twist each strip four or five times to create a corkscrew shape, pressing down on the ends to keep the dough twisted. (Alternatively, transfer the flat dough strips to the baking sheets and don't twist them.) Mist the breadsticks with olive oil, cover loosely with plastic wrap, and let them rise until they puff up a little, about 20 minutes.

4. Sprinkle the breadsticks with salt. Bake, rotating the baking sheets once from front to back and top to bottom, until the breadsticks are golden brown and crisp, 10 to 15 minutes. Transfer the breadsticks to a cooling rack; they will become crisper as they cool. Repeat the rolling, rising, and baking process with the remaining dough.

GET AHEAD: Store in an airtight container at room temperature for up to 2 days. Reheat on a baking sheet in a 350°F [180°C] oven for 5 minutes to refresh, if desired.

This spongy flatbread or pancake, called injera *in Ethiopia and Eritrea, doubles as both bread and an eating utensil—you use the bread to pick up bites of stew with your hands. Traditionally, the bread is made with 100 percent teff flour—an ancient grain with a lovely toasty cocoa-bitter flavor and aroma. I add a little all-purpose flour to make the breads a bit sturdier and easier to flip. Normally the batter is fermented for 24 hours or so to give the bread its characteristic spongy texture and pleasantly sour flavor; I use beer for a similar bubbly texture and plain yogurt for sour tang, so the bread batter is ready to go in 5 minutes flat. These breads reheat well, so you can make them a few days ahead.*

MAKES

8

BREADS

SERVES

4 TO 6

ACTIVE TIME

10

MINUTES

TOTAL TIME

15

MINUTES

Savory Teff Pancakes

PAIR WITH

Spicy Ethiopian Red Lentil Soup (PAGE 51)

¾ cup plus 1 Tbsp [130 g] teff flour
½ cup [70 g] all-purpose flour
1 Tbsp nutritional yeast
¾ tsp baking soda
½ tsp sea salt
1¼ cups [300 ml] lager beer
(don't measure the foam)
¼ cup plus 2 Tbsp [90 g]
tangy plain yogurt
1 Tbsp safflower oil

1. In a large bowl, whisk together both flours, the nutritional yeast, baking soda, and salt. Add the beer and yogurt and whisk until smooth. The mixture should resemble thin pancake batter. (Depending on the thickness of your chosen yogurt, you may need to add more beer or water to the batter to make it spread easily in the pan. You'll be able to gauge any adjustments after making the first pancake.)

2. Heat a large nonstick pan with a tight-fitting lid over medium-low heat. Brush the pan with a little of the safflower oil, stir the batter, and scoop up ⅓ cup [80 ml] of the batter with a measuring cup or ladle. Take the pan off the heat, and quickly pour the batter into the pan, immediately tilting the pan and rotating it so the batter spreads out into a 10-in [25-cm] pancake. Return the pan to the stove, cover, and cook until the injera is firm and springy to the touch and no longer sticky, about 1½ minutes. Remove the lid and let the bread cook for a few seconds more to evaporate any condensation that has dripped off the lid into the pan.

3. Slide a silicone spatula under the edges of the bread to release it from the pan and flip or slide the pancake onto a dinner plate. Cover the plate tightly with aluminum foil and continue cooking the breads, stirring the batter before cooking the next one, until all the batter is used.

4. Serve the pancakes warm.

GET AHEAD: Stack the cooled pancakes, tightly wrap in foil, and store in the refrigerator for up to 2 days. To reheat, unwrap the breads, wrap them in a few dampened paper towels, and microwave on high for 1 minute, or until heated through.

Called roti jala *in Malaysia, meaning "net bread," these soft, panfried flatbreads are a popular street food, usually served with chicken curry. Roti jala traditionally get their netlike appearance from pouring batter through a special small funnel with multiple holes onto a hot griddle. I use a squeeze bottle instead to "draw" the zigzags of batter in the pan, but you can also dip a fork into the batter and drizzle the batter into the pan. If you're not a stickler for authenticity, pour the batter into the pan to make crêpe-like rounds instead. No matter how you approach them, these tender little curry- and coconut-flavored flatbreads are a delicious addition to any soup meal.*

MAKES
ABOUT

12

BREADS

SERVES

4 TO 5

ACTIVE TIME

25

MINUTES

TOTAL TIME

25

MINUTES

Malaysian Net Breads

PAIR WITH

Spicy Sweet Chicken Curry Soup (PAGE 102)

1 cup [140 g] all-purpose flour
¾ tsp sea salt
1 tsp curry powder
1 cup [240 ml] light coconut milk
1 large egg

1. In a medium bowl, whisk together the flour, salt, and curry powder. Add the coconut milk, ½ cup [120 ml] water, and the egg and whisk until smooth. Pour the batter into a squeeze bottle, if using.

2. Coat a large nonstick skillet with a little cooking spray and place it over medium heat. When the pan is warm, drizzle about 3 Tbsp of the batter in concentric circles and then a zigzag pattern to form a 6-in [15-cm] round. It should look something like a net or spider's web, but don't worry if it's not perfectly round. If you don't have a squeeze bottle, drizzle the batter into the pan with a fork, flicking it from side to side to get the net look. Cook until the top of the roti is dry and the bottom is golden brown, about 1 minute. Flip the bread and cook on the second side for 15 seconds.

3. Fold the bread in half and transfer it to a plate. Cover loosely with aluminum foil and repeat with the remaining batter, adding more cooking spray as needed. Adjust the heat if the breads are beginning to burn.

4. Serve the breads warm.

GET AHEAD: Store the batter in an airtight container in the refrigerator for up to 2 days; whisk well before cooking.

Soda Breads and Skillet Breads

Soda bread is served at nearly every meal in Ireland, and every baker has his or her own version. Mine is based on my grandmother's recipe and includes white whole-wheat flour (an easy-to-love, mild-tasting whole wheat), cold grated butter, buttermilk, and thyme. If you can't find white whole-wheat flour, use equal parts of all-purpose and whole-wheat flours. Instead of baking this recipe as one large loaf, which takes an hour or more, I divvy up the batter into little rolls to expedite things.

Mini-Irish Soda Breads

PAIR WITH

Fast Irish Stew (PAGE 125)

MAKES

12

ROLLS

SERVES

6

ACTIVE TIME

15

MINUTES

TOTAL TIME

35

MINUTES

½ cup [110 g] cold unsalted butter
4 cups [540 g] white
    whole-wheat flour
1 tsp baking soda
1 tsp sea salt
2¼ cups [540 ml] buttermilk,
    plus 1 Tbsp for brushing
1 Tbsp chopped fresh thyme
2 Tbsp rolled oats

1. Preheat the oven to 400°F [200°C]. Line a baking sheet with parchment paper.

2. Grate the butter on the large holes of a box grater and place in the freezer while preparing the remaining ingredients.

3. In a large mixing bowl, whisk together the flour, baking soda, and salt. Add the butter and rub it into the flour mixture with your fingertips until it is in tiny pieces.

4. Add the 2¼ cups [540 ml] buttermilk and thyme to the bowl and stir until they are just incorporated and the mixture comes together into a rough, shaggy dough; don't overmix or the rolls will be tough.

5. Using an ice-cream scoop or ⅓ cup [80-ml] measure, scoop out 12 balls of dough and place them about 1 in [2.5 cm] apart on the prepared baking sheet. Gently pat them into 2½- to 3-in [6- to 7.5-cm] rounds, brush with the remaining 1 Tbsp buttermilk, and sprinkle with the oats. Bake until the rolls are golden brown and a skewer inserted into the center comes out clean, 20 to 25 minutes. Let the breads cool on a wire rack for 5 to 10 minutes.

6. Serve the breads warm or at room temperature.

GET AHEAD: Freeze the unbaked breads on a parchment-lined baking sheet until solid and then store in a zip-top plastic freezer bag for up to 3 months. Bake as many frozen rolls as needed at 400°F [200°C] on a parchment-lined baking sheet until golden brown, about 25 minutes.

MAKES	
12	
DUMPLINGS	

SERVES

6

ACTIVE TIME

10

MINUTES

TOTAL TIME

20

MINUTES

When gently poached in a brothy soup, these dumplings have a light, fluffy texture and delicious flavor, thanks to fresh herbs and lemon zest. All you need is a bowl and a wooden spoon.

Featherlight Herb Dumplings

PAIR WITH

Soulful Chicken Soup (PAGE 96)

1½ cups [210 g] all-purpose flour
½ cup [70 g] fine cornmeal
2 tsp baking powder
1 tsp sea salt
3 Tbsp cold unsalted butter,
    cut into ¼-in [6-mm] cubes
1 cup [240 ml] milk
2 Tbsp finely chopped mixed fresh
    herbs (such as parsley, chives,
    dill, tarragon, thyme, and basil)
2 tsp finely grated lemon zest

1. In a large bowl, whisk together the flour, cornmeal, baking powder, and salt. Add the butter and rub it into the flour mixture with your fingertips until the mixture resembles fine granola. Add the milk, herbs, and lemon zest and stir with a wooden spoon until the mixture just comes together and there are no traces of dry flour. Don't overmix or the dumplings will be tough.

2. Drop the batter by the heaping tablespoon into gently simmering soup or stew. Cover and cook until a skewer inserted into the center of the largest dumpling comes out clean, 10 to 12 minutes.

3. Serve the dumplings and soup immediately.

GET AHEAD: The flour and butter mixture can be made ahead and refrigerated for up to 2 weeks. To finish the dumplings, follow the instructions as directed.

MAKES

1

CORNBREAD

SERVES

8

ACTIVE TIME

10

MINUTES

TOTAL TIME

35

MINUTES

This rustic corn bread has a hearty whole-grain texture thanks to blue cornmeal (look for it in the bulk section of natural food stores) and white whole-wheat flour. You can substitute regular cornmeal if blue cornmeal is unavailable. The hint of sweetness comes from maple syrup; use Grade A dark maple syrup for the richest flavor. Because this bread has a hint of sweetness and a rustic texture, it complements spicy, robust fare like the Jamaican stew on page 120 and the Cincinnati chili on page 110.

Blue Corn and Maple Skillet Bread

PAIR WITH

Jamaican Pork and Sweet Potato Stew (PAGE 120)
Four-Way Cincinnati Chili (PAGE 110)

6 Tbsp [85 g] unsalted butter
1 cup [140 g] blue cornmeal
1 cup [140 g] white whole-wheat flour
1 Tbsp baking powder
¾ tsp sea salt
¾ cup [180 ml] buttermilk
½ cup [120 g] sour cream or plain
   full-fat Greek yogurt
3 Tbsp Grade A dark amber
   maple syrup
2 large eggs

1. Preheat the oven to 425°F [220°C]. While the oven is heating up, place the butter in a 12-in [30.5-cm] cast-iron skillet, slide the skillet into the oven, and heat the pan until the butter has melted, about 10 minutes. Remove the skillet from the oven.

2. In a large bowl, whisk together the cornmeal, flour, baking powder, and salt. In a medium bowl, whisk together the buttermilk, sour cream, maple syrup, and eggs. Add the buttermilk mixture to the cornmeal mixture and scrape the melted butter from the skillet into the batter. Mix with a wooden spoon until just blended. Do not overmix.

3. Scrape the batter into the skillet and smooth the top with a rubber spatula. Bake until a skewer inserted into the center comes out clean, 20 to 25 minutes. Let the bread cool in the pan for 5 to 10 minutes.

4. Cut the corn bread into wedges. Serve warm or at room temperature.

GET AHEAD: This moist corn bread freezes well. Stack the cooled wedges, wrap them in foil, and freeze in a zip-top plastic freezer bag for up to 3 months. To reheat, arrange the bread in an even layer on a baking sheet, cover with foil, and bake in a 350°F [180°C] oven until heated through, 15 to 20 minutes.

Bannock bread is a quick skillet bread that uses everyday pantry ingredients and can be cooked over a campfire—thus its popularity with early Scottish and Irish pioneers. Oat flour gives the bread a soft, spongy inside while butter and eggs give the bread a rich, crispy exterior. Look for oat flour in the bulk section of natural food stores, or make your own for this recipe by pulsing ¼ cup plus 2 Tbsp [35 g] of rolled oats in a food processor until finely ground.

Bannock bread is an ideal dipper for brothy soups, and when toasted lightly, it makes delicious croutons to float in soup as well. The crispy sage leaves and browned butter in the batter give this golden bread a lovely earthy autumn flavor, so any soup with mushrooms, winter squash, or sage will partner well.

Bannock Bread with Browned Butter and Sage

PAIR WITH

Pumpkin, Pancetta, and Arborio Rice Soup (PAGE 68)
Creamy Wild Rice and Turkey Soup (PAGE 106)

MAKES

1

BREAD

SERVES

6 TO **8**

ACTIVE TIME

10

MINUTES

TOTAL TIME

30

MINUTES

⅓ cup [80 g] unsalted butter, cut into ¼-in [6-mm] cubes
8 to 10 large fresh sage leaves
1⅓ cups [185 g] unbleached all-purpose flour
⅓ cup [40 g] oat flour
1 Tbsp sugar
½ tsp baking powder
¼ tsp baking soda
½ tsp sea salt
1 cup [240 ml] buttermilk
3 large eggs, beaten

1. Preheat the oven to 425°F [220°C]. While the oven is heating up, place the butter and sage in a heavy 12- to 14-in [30.5- to 35.5-cm] cast-iron skillet, slide the skillet into the oven, and cook until the butter is browned and the sage is crispy, about 15 minutes. Remove the skillet from the oven. Carefully remove the sage from the skillet, trying to keep the leaves whole, and set them aside. Let the butter cool in the pan a little while you make the batter.

2. In a large bowl, whisk together both flours, the sugar, baking powder, baking soda, and salt. Add the buttermilk and eggs to the dry ingredients and scrape the melted butter from the skillet into the batter. Stir with a wooden spoon until just combined and there are no traces of dry flour in the batter. Do not overmix.

3. Scrape the batter into the skillet, smooth the top with a rubber spatula, and arrange the sage leaves on the top of the batter in a circle. Bake until the bread is golden brown and a skewer inserted into the center comes out clean, about 20 minutes.

4. Cut the bread into wedges and serve warm.

GET AHEAD: Cool the bread completely, wrap in foil, and store at room temperature for up to 2 days. To reheat, open up the top of the foil and put the bread in a 350°F [180°C] oven until it is warmed through, about 10 minutes.

MAKES

8

SCONES

SERVES

8

ACTIVE TIME

10

MINUTES

TOTAL TIME

35

MINUTES

Though most people are familiar only with sweet scones served at teatime, they can also be made savory. In this recipe, I stir baby spinach and sun-dried tomatoes into the dough for color and flavor. I love these scones with soup—they're sturdy enough to use as a dipping device and crunchy enough to crumble over the top as croutons. The raw scones freeze very well, so you can bake only what you need and freeze the rest, so that fresh-baked scones will be at your fingertips.

Spinach and Sun-Dried Tomato Scones

PAIR WITH

Roasted Asparagus Soup with Cashew Cream (PAGE 30)
Black Bean Soup with Roasted Red Pepper Cream (PAGE 54)

1½ cups plus 2 Tbsp [230 g]
    all-purpose flour
2 Tbsp packed brown sugar
2 tsp baking powder
½ tsp baking soda
½ tsp sea salt
¼ tsp freshly ground black pepper
½ cup [110 g] cold unsalted butter,
    cut into ¼-in [6-mm] dice
¼ cup [60 ml] buttermilk
1 large egg
1 cup [40 g] baby spinach, chopped
¼ cup [35 g] sun-dried tomatoes
    packed in oil, drained and chopped

1. Preheat the oven to 400°F [200°C]. Line a baking sheet with parchment paper.

2. In the bowl of a food processor, combine the flour, brown sugar, baking powder, baking soda, salt, and pepper and pulse to combine. Add the butter and pulse until the butter is in tiny flecks, about fifteen 1-second pulses. In a small bowl, whisk together the buttermilk and egg until well combined. Add the buttermilk mixture to the flour mixture and pulse a few times until the flour is just moistened and still crumbly. Add the spinach and sun-dried tomatoes and pulse until the mixture just comes together; do not overmix. (Alternatively, place the dry ingredients in a large bowl and whisk to combine. Add the butter and use a pastry blender or your fingertips to cut the butter into the flour. With a rubber spatula, stir in the buttermilk mixture and then the spinach and sun-dried tomatoes.)

CONTINUED

3. Turn out the dough onto a lightly floured surface and gently pat into an 8-in [20-cm] round about ½ in [12 mm] thick. Cut the dough into eight wedges and use a bench scraper or spatula to transfer the unbaked scones to the prepared baking sheet, placing them about 1 in [2.5 cm] apart. Bake until the scones are crisp and golden brown, and a skewer inserted into the center of one comes out clean, 20 to 25 minutes. Let cool on a wire rack for 5 minutes.

4. Serve the scones warm or at room temperature.

GET AHEAD: The unbaked scones can be frozen on a baking sheet until solid, transferred to a zip-top plastic freezer bag, and frozen for up to 3 months. Bake as directed, adding an additional 5 to 10 minutes.

Baked scones can be wrapped in aluminum foil and stored in the refrigerator for up to 2 days. Reheat, wrapped in foil, in a 350°F [180°C] oven until warm, about 15 minutes.

The cheesy, yeasty flavor of this savory quick bread isn't from yeast, but rather from extra-sharp Cheddar cheese, Dijon mustard, and craft beer (choose your favorite citrusy, hoppy pale ale). It's probably more accurate to call this "Cheddar and beer bread"; the ample cheese in and on top of the bread melts and becomes enticingly crisp around the edges. The recipe makes two smallish loaves, which bake in 30 minutes, rather than one big loaf that would require an hour. You can also use the batter for savory muffins. This bread is best if it's not piping hot; in fact, the flavor improves with age, and it's wonderful toasted.

Beer and Cheddar Bread

PAIR WITH

Smoky San Marzano Tomato Soup (PAGE 34)
Lighter Broccoli and Cheese Soup (PAGE 38)

MAKES
2
LOAVES
OR
12
MUFFINS

SERVES
6 TO **8**

ACTIVE TIME
10
MINUTES

TOTAL TIME
40
MINUTES

1½ cups [210 g] all-purpose flour
1½ cups [210 g] white
  whole-wheat flour
3 Tbsp sugar
1 Tbsp baking powder
1 tsp sea salt
12 oz [354 ml] hoppy craft ale
2 Tbsp Dijon mustard
¼ cup [7 g] minced chives or
  green onion
1½ cups [120 g] grated sharp
  Cheddar cheese

1. Preheat the oven to 350°F [180°C]. Coat two 4-by-8-in [10-by-20-cm] loaf pans or a standard twelve-well muffin tin with nonstick cooking spray.

2. In a large bowl, whisk together both flours, the sugar, baking powder, and salt.

In a small bowl, whisk together the beer, mustard, and chives. Add the beer mixture to the flour mixture. Add ½ cup [40 g] of the cheese and blend the batter with a rubber spatula until just combined. Do not overmix or the breads will be tough.

3. Divide the batter among the prepared loaf pans (the batter will fill the loaf pans less than halfway) or muffin wells and sprinkle the remaining 1 cup [80 g] of cheese on top. Bake until the breads or muffins are golden brown and a skewer inserted into the center comes out clean, 30 to 35 minutes for loaves, and 20 to 25 minutes for muffins. Let cool on a cooling rack for 10 minutes before removing them from the pans.

4. Serve the loaves or muffins warm or at room temperature.

GET AHEAD: Store tightly wrapped in foil in the refrigerator for up to 4 days or in the freezer for up to 3 months. To reheat, defrost overnight. Slice and toast the bread until crusty and warm, about 6 minutes in a toaster or about 3 minutes per side under a broiler, or about 10 minutes in a moderate oven for muffins.

Muffins, Rolls, and Biscuits

Called idli, *these little steamed breads are often served for breakfast alongside* lentil *sambar (see page 47) in southern India. Idli are made with a variety of ingredients—from complicated fermented rice and lentil concoctions to simple preparations like this one, made with plain farina (such as Cream of Wheat). Idli are traditionally steamed in purpose-built metal molds, but it's much easier to microwave them in ramekins.*

MAKES

12

BREADS

SERVES

6

ACTIVE TIME

10

MINUTES

TOTAL TIME

20

MINUTES

Indian Steamed Rice Cakes

PAIR WITH

South Indian Sambar (PAGE 47)

**3 Tbsp melted coconut oil or
    safflower oil
1 tsp brown mustard seeds
½ tsp cumin seeds
2 tsp minced fresh ginger
1 serrano chile, finely chopped
1 cup [170 g] farina
⅓ cup [80 g] plain yogurt
3 Tbsp chopped fresh cilantro
¼ tsp baking soda
½ tsp sea salt**

1. Heat 2 Tbsp of the coconut oil in a medium sauté pan over medium heat. Add the mustard seeds and cumin seeds and cook until they begin to pop, about 20 seconds. Add the ginger and serrano and sauté until fragrant, another 30 seconds.

2. Add the farina to the pan and cook, stirring constantly, until it smells toasty, about 2 minutes. Transfer the mixture to a medium bowl. Add 1 cup [240 ml] water, the yogurt, cilantro, baking soda, and salt and whisk thoroughly until there are no lumps.

3. Brush 12 small (1½-oz/45-ml capacity) microwave-safe ramekins (I use soy sauce dipping dishes) with the remaining 1 Tbsp coconut oil. Spoon about 2 Tbsp of batter into each ramekin and arrange them closely together in the microwave. Dampen a small wad of paper towels with water and place it alongside (but not touching) the ramekins; this will create steam, which will help cook the breads. Microwave on high for 2 minutes. (Alternatively, place the ramekins in a two-level bamboo steamer with a lid and steam the breads over boiling water for about 10 minutes. You may need to do this in batches, depending on the size of your steamer. Wrap the first batch of steamed idli in foil to keep them warm while steaming the second batch.)

4. Check for doneness by pressing the tops of the idli; they should be firm (not liquid) to the touch. If any idli are liquid in places, rearrange them and microwave on high in 30-second intervals (or steam them) until completely cooked.

5. Run a knife around each idli and turn them out onto a serving plate. Serve the idli warm.

GET AHEAD: Store the idli in an airtight container in the refrigerator for up to 3 days. To reheat, arrange on a plate, cover with a few damp paper towels, and microwave on high until heated through, about 30 seconds. Alternatively, you can steam the idli on a lightly oiled steamer rack.

MAKES

12

BISCUITS

SERVES

12

ACTIVE TIME

10

MINUTES

TOTAL TIME

20

MINUTES

Soft, cheesy, and super easy to make, these one-bowl biscuits taste just like pimento cheese—the roasted red pepper and Cheddar cheese spread adored in the South. I love to dunk them into soups from the same region, especially gumbos of any kind and red beans and rice soup.

To make gluten-free pimento cheese biscuits, substitute 2 cups [310 g] of King Arthur Gluten Free Flour Blend for the all-purpose flour and proceed as directed.

Pimento Cheese Drop Biscuits

<u>PAIR WITH</u>

Sausage Gumbo (PAGE 116)
Cajun Red Beans and Rice Soup (PAGE 61)

2 cups [280 g] all-purpose flour
1 Tbsp baking powder
2 tsp sugar
¾ tsp sea salt
1 tsp sweet paprika
1 cup [240 ml] milk
¼ cup [60 g] mayonnaise
1 cup [80 g] shredded sharp
   Cheddar cheese
3 Tbsp finely chopped jarred roasted
   red peppers, patted dry

1. Preheat the oven to 450°F [230°C]. Line a baking sheet with parchment paper and coat with cooking spray.

2. In a large bowl, whisk together the flour, baking powder, sugar, salt, and paprika. Add the milk and mayonnaise and stir with a rubber spatula until the flour mixture is just moistened, about fifteen strokes. Fold in the cheese and roasted red peppers until just combined.

3. Using a small ice-cream scoop or ¼-cup [60-ml] measure, scoop out the batter and drop onto the prepared baking sheet, spacing the raw biscuits about 3 in [7.5 cm] apart. Bake until the biscuits are golden brown, 10 to 12 minutes. Let cool for 5 to 10 minutes on a wire rack.

4. Serve the biscuits warm or at room temperature.

<u>GET AHEAD:</u> Store the cooled biscuits in an airtight container in the refrigerator for up to 2 days. Or freeze the unbaked biscuits on a parchment-lined baking sheet until firm, transfer to a zip-top plastic freezer bag, and freeze for up to 3 months. Reheat the refrigerated biscuits on a baking sheet in a 400°F [200°C] oven until warm, about 8 minutes, or bake the frozen dough on a parchment-lined baking sheet until golden brown, 15 to 20 minutes.

MAKES

6

EGG BREADS

SERVES

6

ACTIVE TIME

10

MINUTES

TOTAL TIME

30

MINUTES

These rolls, called gyeranbang, are a favorite street food during the cold winters in Korea. The rich, somewhat sweet batter is cooked in special cast-iron molds, with a whole egg cracked over the top of each bread. In lieu of the specialized pan, I bake the rolls in a jumbo muffin tin to accommodate the large eggs I usually have on hand. If you have only a standard-size muffin tin, make the batter as directed with 2 large eggs, and then crack a medium egg on top of the batter in each well, so the eggs won't overflow. The egg breads are great with Asian soups and make a terrific grab-and-go breakfast, too!

Korean Egg Breads

PAIR WITH

Korean Kimchi and Tofu Soup (PAGE 37)
Barbecue Pork and Miso Ramen (PAGE 118)

½ cup [110 g] unsalted butter,
    melted and cooled slightly
¼ cup [60 ml] milk
2 Tbsp sugar
1 tsp dark sesame oil
8 large eggs
¾ cup plus 2 Tbsp [125 g]
    all-purpose flour
1¼ tsp baking powder
¼ tsp sea salt
1 green onion, thinly sliced

1. Preheat the oven to 350°F [180°C]. Coat a jumbo six-well muffin tin with cooking spray.

2. In a blender or food processor, combine the butter, milk, sugar, sesame oil, and 2 eggs and blend until smooth. In a medium bowl, whisk together the flour, baking powder, and salt. Add the flour mixture to the blender or food processor and blend until smooth, stopping once or twice to scrape down the sides.

3. Pour the batter into the prepared muffin wells (about 2 Tbsp per well). Break 1 egg over the batter in each well, and sprinkle the green onion over the top. Bake until a skewer inserted into the center of the bread comes out clean and the egg is set, about 20 minutes.

4. Let the breads rest in the tin for 5 minutes. Run a knife around the edges of the breads to loosen them from the tin.

5. Serve the egg breads immediately, while still warm.

GET AHEAD: Though best hot out of the oven, the breads can be cooled and stored, individually wrapped in plastic in the refrigerator for up to 4 days. Allow them to come to room temperature or microwave on high heat for 20 seconds before serving. The breads cannot be frozen.

Homemade dinner rolls are one of life's simple pleasures. And though you can easily find recipes that take hours (or several days), these rich, yeasty rolls can be made with only 10 minutes of prep and 30 minutes of rising time. To gild the lily just a bit, I wrap the rolls in prosciutto, which forms a crispy outer shell, and crown them with chopped green olives for a salty, fruity hit. If you're serving vegetarians, omit the prosciutto.

Olive and Prosciutto Rolls

PAIR WITH

Spicy Sicilian Clam Soup with Fregola (PAGE 82)
Italian Meatball and Greens Soup (PAGE 104)

MAKES
12
ROLLS

SERVES
12

ACTIVE TIME
10
MINUTES

TOTAL TIME
50
MINUTES

6 thin slices prosciutto
1 recipe Fresh-and-Fast Olive Oil Bread Dough (page 20), or 1 lb [455 g] packaged fresh pizza dough
12 Castelvetrano or other green olives, pitted and sliced
2 Tbsp extra-virgin olive oil
Flaky sea salt
Freshly ground black pepper

1. Preheat the oven to 425°F [220°C]. Coat a twelve-well muffin tin with cooking spray.

2. Tear the prosciutto slices in half lengthwise and place them around the insides of the prepared muffin wells. Tear the dough into twelve equal pieces and place them in the muffin wells. Push the olives into the tops of the dough, drizzle each one with 1 tsp of the olive oil, and sprinkle with salt and pepper. Cover loosely with plastic wrap and set aside in a warm place for 30 minutes to rise; the rolls should double in size and look puffy.

3. Uncover the rolls. Bake until the rolls are golden brown, 18 to 20 minutes. Let the rolls cool in the pan for 5 minutes, then use a butter knife to gently pry them from the muffin wells.

4. Serve the rolls warm or at room temperature.

GET AHEAD: Store the cooled rolls in an airtight container in the refrigerator for up to 2 days. Or wrap them individually in plastic wrap, slip into zip-top plastic freezer bags, and store in the freezer for up to 3 months. Reheat, wrapped in foil, in a 350°F [180°C] oven until warm, about 10 minutes for refrigerated rolls and 20 minutes for frozen rolls.

Called pão de queijo, *or "cheese bread" in Portuguese, these little rolls are the sexy South American cousins of the chic* gougères *on page 166; but they rely on tapioca flour instead of wheat flour, so they're gluten-free. They're a little spicy thanks to the jalapeño and nicely salty from Asiago cheese, so they work well with soups that have a little spice, like the seafood and coconut soup on page 80 and the black bean soup with red pepper cream on page 54.*

MAKES

24

PUFFS

SERVES

6

ACTIVE TIME

10

MINUTES

TOTAL TIME

30

MINUTES

Brazilian Tapioca and Cheese Rolls

PAIR WITH

Brazilian Seafood and Coconut Soup (PAGE 80)
Black Bean Soup with Roasted Red Pepper Cream (PAGE 54)

⅓ cup [80 ml] milk
¼ cup [50 g] coconut oil
¼ tsp sea salt
¾ cup [85 g] tapioca flour
1 large egg, beaten
½ cup [45 g] shredded Asiago cheese
1 Tbsp finely chopped jalapeño or
    Fresno chile

1. Preheat the oven to 400°F [200°C]. Coat two twelve-well mini muffin tins with cooking spray and place the tins on a rimmed baking sheet.

2. In a microwave-safe measuring cup with a spout, combine the milk, coconut oil, and salt. Microwave on high until the coconut oil has melted and the milk is hot to the touch, about 1 minute.

3. Place the tapioca flour in a food processor and, with the machine running, gradually add the milk mixture. Scrape down the sides of the work bowl and let the mixture stand, uncovered, for 5 minutes to cool.

4. Replace the processor's lid and, with the machine running, pour the egg through the feed tube. Stop and scrape the sides again. Add the cheese and jalapeño and pulse a few times to combine all the ingredients (about ten 1-second pulses).

5. Pour a scant 1 Tbsp of the batter into each of the prepared muffin wells. Bake, rotating the pan once, until the rolls are puffed up and golden brown, 15 to 20 minutes. Cool the puffs in the pan for 5 minutes.

6. Serve the puffs warm.

GET AHEAD: Store the baked rolls in zip-top plastic freezer bags in the freezer for up to 3 months. To reheat, wrap the frozen rolls loosely in aluminum foil and bake in a 350°F [180°C] oven until heated through, about 15 minutes.

MAKES

24

PUFFS

SERVES

6

PREP TIME

15

MINUTES

TOTAL TIME

45

MINUTES

This simple choux pastry dough—made of milk, butter, flour, eggs, and Gruyère cheese—comes together quickly. Once baked, the airy little puffballs (called gougères in French) are so full of nutty cheese flavor that they are all but impossible to stop eating. You can substitute any full-flavored cheese for the Gruyère—Parmigiano-Reggiano, Pecorino Toscano, and Spanish Idiazabal come to mind.

Gruyère Cheese Choux Pastry Puffs

PAIR WITH

Crab Buttermilk Bisque with Sweet Corn and Bacon (PAGE 73)
Lobster Tail Bisque (PAGE 76)

¼ cup [60 ml] whole milk
4 tablespoons [55 g] unsalted butter, cut into pieces
¼ tsp sea salt
½ cup [70 g] all-purpose flour
2 large eggs, at room temperature
1 cup [85g] grated Gruyère or other aged cheese (see headnote)

1. Preheat the oven to 425°F [220°C]. Line a baking sheet with parchment paper.

2. In a medium saucepan over high heat, bring the milk, ¼ cup [60 ml] water, the butter, and the salt to a boil. Remove the pan from the heat, add the flour all at once, and stir to combine. Place the pan over medium-low heat and stir vigorously with a wooden spoon to dry out the dough, 3 to 5 minutes. The dough is ready when it is glossy and stiff enough to hold a spoon upright.

3. Transfer the dough to a large bowl and beat with a hand mixer on medium speed, or beat in a stand mixer until the dough is no longer steaming, about 2 minutes.

Add one of the eggs, beating until completely incorporated into the dough. Add the second egg, and beat until the dough is thick and shiny. Add the grated cheese and beat until the cheese has been thoroughly incorporated.

4. Using two wet soupspoons, spoon 1-in [2.5-cm] mounds onto the prepared baking sheet, spacing them about 2 in [5 cm] apart. Bake the puffs for 5 minutes. Lower the oven temperature to 375°F [190°C] and continue baking until the puffs are browned and cooked through, 15 to 18 minutes. Test for doneness by quickly retrieving one puff from the oven (close the oven door and continue to bake the remaining puffs). Let the test puff rest for 30 seconds on a cutting board; if it starts to deflate, the puffs are not sufficiently baked. Cut the puff in half—the center should be a little moist, but not wet to the touch. Continue to bake the remaining puffs for a few more minutes, if necessary.

5. Serve the puffs immediately.

GET AHEAD: The unbaked puffs can be frozen on a baking sheet until firm, transferred to a zip-top plastic bag, and frozen for up to 3 months. Bake while frozen, adding an additional 2 to 5 minutes to the baking time.

This is easily my favorite corn bread recipe of all time and it just happens to be gluten-free. The combination of sweet rice flour and cornmeal makes these muffins exceptionally light, and the addition of Parmigiano-Reggiano gives them a savory umami boost. For the most tender muffins, use fine-ground yellow cornmeal, not the medium-ground cornmeal that's used for polenta and grits. If you can't find the finer grind, whiz medium-ground cornmeal in a clean spice grinder or a high-powered blender until finely ground.

Gluten-Free Corn Muffins

<u>PAIR WITH</u>

Roasted Beet and Carrot Soup (PAGE 32)

MAKES

MUFFINS

SERVES

ACTIVE TIME

8

MINUTES

TOTAL TIME

30

MINUTES

1 cup [140 g] sweet rice flour
1 cup [140 g] fine-ground yellow cornmeal (I use Albers Mill Yellow Cornmeal)
¼ cup [8 g] finely grated Parmigiano-Reggiano cheese
2 Tbsp chopped fresh thyme
1½ Tbsp sugar
2½ tsp baking powder
¾ tsp sea salt
1¼ cups [300 ml] buttermilk
2 large eggs
3 Tbsp unsalted butter, melted and cooled

1. Preheat the oven to 375°F [190°C]. Coat a standard twelve-well muffin tin with cooking spray.

2. In a large bowl, whisk together the rice flour, cornmeal, cheese, thyme, sugar, baking powder, and salt. In a medium bowl, whisk together the buttermilk, eggs, and butter. Add the buttermilk mixture to the flour mixture and stir until just blended; a few lumps are fine.

3. Using an ice-cream scoop, divide the batter among the prepared muffin wells, filling them about two-thirds full. Bake, rotating the tin once, until a skewer inserted into the center of a muffin comes out clean, 20 to 25 minutes. Cool the muffins in the pan on a cooling rack for 5 minutes before removing.

4. Serve the muffins warm or at room temperature.

<u>GET AHEAD:</u> Store the cooled muffins in an airtight container in the refrigerator for up to 3 days, or wrap individually in plastic wrap, slip into zip-top plastic freezer bags, and store in the freezer for up to 3 months. To reheat, microwave for 1 minute on high if refrigerated, or 2 minutes if frozen. Or wrap in aluminum foil and reheat in a 350°F [180°C] oven until warmed, 10 minutes for refrigerated muffins and 20 minutes for frozen muffins.

Grated zucchini keeps these muffins moist, while salty feta cheese and dill give them a savory character. They're perfect partners for Mediterranean soups like the yogurt and bulgur soup on page 62 or the Greek egg and lemon soup with orzo pictured here (recipe on page 94). These muffins are on the small side, so I usually serve two per person.

Zucchini, Feta, and Dill Muffins

PAIR WITH

Persian Yogurt, Lentil, and Bulgur Soup
with Browned Herb Butter (PAGE 62)
Egg and Lemon Soup with Toasted Orzo and Kale (PAGE 94)

1½ cups [210 g] all-purpose flour
2¼ tsp baking powder
¾ tsp sea salt
¾ cup [180 ml] milk
1 large egg
1 medium zucchini, grated
½ cup [85 g] crumbled feta cheese
5 Tbsp [70 g] unsalted butter,
    melted, or 5 Tbsp [75 ml]
    extra-virgin olive oil
3 Tbsp chopped fresh dill

1. Preheat the oven to 400°F [200°C]. Coat a twelve-well muffin tin with cooking spray.

2. In a large mixing bowl, whisk together the flour, baking powder, and salt. In a medium bowl, whisk together the milk and egg. Pour the milk mixture into the flour mixture, and add the zucchini, cheese, butter, and dill. Stir until just blended, about fifteen strokes (a few lumps are okay).

3. Using an ice-cream scoop or ⅓ cup [75 ml] measuring cup, fill the prepared muffin wells two-thirds full with batter. Bake, rotating the tin once, until a skewer inserted into the center of a muffin comes out clean, about 25 minutes. Transfer to a cooling rack and let the muffins cool in the tin for 5 minutes before removing.

4. Serve the muffins warm or at room temperature.

GET AHEAD: Store in an airtight container in the refrigerator for up to 3 days. Or wrap individually in plastic wrap, slip into zip-top plastic freezer bags, and store in the freezer for up to 1 month. To serve refrigerated muffins, unwrap them and microwave on high for 10 to 30 seconds, or until warm in the center, or wrap in foil and bake in a 350°F [180°C] oven until heated through, 20 to 25 minutes. For frozen muffins, microwave on high for 2 minutes or wrap in foil and bake until heated through, about 35 minutes.

MAKES

12

MUFFINS

SERVES

12

ACTIVE TIME

15

MINUTES

TOTAL TIME

40

MINUTES

These easy whole-grain muffins are extra moist, thanks to the grated onion, which also adds a savory sweetness. The seed topping is in homage to "everything" bagels with all those lovely seeds and fried shallot bits, so it follows that they're just as good with soup as they are smeared with cream cheese for breakfast the next day.

Everything Rye Muffins

PAIR WITH

Roasted Cauliflower and Paprika Soup (PAGE 40)
Friulian Bean and Sauerkraut Soup (PAGE 58)

3 tsp toasted caraway seeds
2 tsp chia seeds or poppy seeds
1 tsp fennel seeds
2 tsp fried shallots (see Flavor Toolbox, page 14) or dried onion flakes
2 tsp dried minced garlic (available in the bulk spice section of supermarkets)
1⅓ cups [145 g] dark rye flour
1 cup [140 g] white whole-wheat flour
2½ tsp baking powder
1 tsp ground coriander
1 tsp sea salt
½ tsp baking soda
1½ cups [360 ml] buttermilk
¼ cup [35 g] grated yellow onion
1 large egg
1 Tbsp molasses
4 Tbsp [55 g] unsalted butter, melted

1. Preheat the oven to 375°F [190°C]. Coat a twelve-well muffin tin with cooking spray.

2. In a small bowl, combine 1 tsp of the caraway seeds, the chia seeds, fennel seeds, fried shallots, and dried garlic and set aside. In a large bowl, whisk together both flours, the baking powder, the remaining 2 tsp caraway seeds, coriander, salt, and baking soda. In a medium bowl, whisk together the buttermilk, onion, egg, and molasses. Make a well in the center of the flour mixture and add the buttermilk mixture. Add the butter and stir with a wooden spoon until just combined. Some lumps are okay; you don't want to stir too much or the muffins will be tough.

3. Scoop the batter into the prepared muffin wells (they will be about three-quarters full) and sprinkle with the seed mixture. Bake until the muffins are golden brown on top and a skewer inserted into the largest muffin comes out clean, about 25 minutes. Cool in the pan on a wire rack for 10 minutes. Remove the muffins from the pan.

4. Serve warm or at room temperature.

GET AHEAD: Store the cooled muffins in an airtight container at room temperature for up to 3 days, or in zip-top plastic freezer bags in the freezer for up to 3 months. Reheat, wrapped loosely in foil, in a 350°F [180°C] oven until warmed through, 10 minutes for room-temperature muffins and 20 minutes for frozen muffins.

Protein-rich quinoa flour gives these muffins a pleasingly grassy flavor, while grated apple keeps them moist and a little sweet. Look for quinoa flour in the bulk section of natural food stores, or in boxes in the baking aisle of supermarkets. You can make this a gluten-free bread by replacing the all-purpose flour with 1 cup [175 g] gluten-free flour. I like King Arthur's all-purpose gluten-free blend.

Quinoa doesn't mess around; it gives baked goods a fairly assertive whole-grain flavor, so pair these muffins with soups with bold flavors, like the mushroom and quinoa soup on page 65 or the roasted poblano and potato chowder on page 48.

MAKES

12
MUFFINS

SERVES

12

ACTIVE TIME

10
MINUTES

TOTAL TIME

35
MINUTES

Quinoa, Apple, and Cheddar Muffins

PAIR WITH

Many Mushroom and Quinoa Soup (PAGE 65)
Spicy Roasted Poblano and Potato Chowder (PAGE 48)

1 cup [140 g] quinoa flour
1 cup [140 g] all-purpose flour
1 Tbsp plus 1 tsp baking powder
¾ tsp sea salt
1 cup [240 ml] buttermilk
1 cup [120 g] grated unpeeled
 Fuji apple
2 large eggs
2 Tbsp extra-virgin olive oil
¼ cup [7 g] minced fresh chives
 or green onion
1 cup [80 g] grated aged Cheddar
 cheese

1. Preheat the oven to 375°F [190°C]. Coat a twelve-well muffin tin with cooking spray.

2. In a large bowl, whisk together both flours, the baking powder, and the salt. In a medium bowl, whisk together the buttermilk, apple, eggs, olive oil, and chives. Add the buttermilk mixture to the flour mixture. Add half of the cheese and mix with a wooden spoon until the dry ingredients are just moistened.

3. Spoon the batter into the prepared muffin wells and sprinkle with the remaining cheese. Bake until the tops are golden brown and a skewer inserted into the center comes out clean, 20 to 25 minutes. Cool the muffins in the pan on a rack for 10 minutes before removing.

4. Serve the muffins warm or at room temperature.

GET AHEAD: Store the muffins in an airtight container in the refrigerator for up to 4 days, or wrap them individually in plastic wrap and store in zip-top plastic bags in the freezer for up to 3 months. To reheat, wrap in foil and place in a 350°F [180°C] oven until warmed throughout, about 10 minutes for refrigerated muffins and 20 minutes for frozen muffins.

Acknowledgments

This book was a joy to work on not only because I got to surround my family and friends with the homespun comforts of soup and bread but also because I got to work with home cooks and pros who love the combo as much as I do. A heaping ladleful of thanks goes out to all of the soup lovers and home bakers who contributed to this book: Rebecca Gagnon, Jacki Thau, Mora Chatarand, Cathie Schutz, Don Lesser, Susan Gilbertson, Kathleen Bauer, and Seamus Foran. I also would like to raise my soupspoon in gratitude to my husband, Gregor Torrence, for his support and expert tasting and feedback.

Thanks also to my agent, Jenny Ferrari-Adler, for her help and encouragement; Amy Treadwell for shepherding this book to fruition; and Deanne Katz for her tireless guidance, good humor, and appreciation of Nigel Tufnel. Heaps of gratitude to the rest of the Chronicle Books team, food stylist Ashley Marti, and photographer Dina Avila for helping me put this all down on paper and making it look so very pretty.

Index